DAVID RAVENHILL

OVERCOMING
THE ENEMY'S PLANS
to DESTROY YOUR LIFE

DAVID RAVENHILL

OVERCOMING
THE ENEMY'S PLANS
to DESTROY YOUR LIFE

Offspring
PUBLISHERS

www.offspringpublishers.com

Overcoming the Enemy's Plans to Destroy Your Life, Copyright © 2022 by David Ravenhill. Editing, cover and interior design by Cheryl Sasai Ellicott.

All rights reserved. No part of this document may be reproduced or transmitted in any form, by any means (electronic, photocopying, recording, or otherwise) without the written permission of the author.

Unless otherwise indicated, Bible quotations are taken from the New American Standard Bible (NASB), Copyright © 1960, 1962, 1963, 1968, 1971, 1972, 1973, 1975, 1977, 1995 by The Lockman Foundation.

Scripture quotations marked (NLT) are taken from the *Holy Bible,* New Living Translation, copyright © 1996, 2004, 2015 by Tyndale House Foundation. Used by permission of Tyndale House Publishers, Carol Stream, Illinois 60188, USA. All rights reserved.

Bible quotations marked KJV are taken from the King James Version of the Bible. Public domain.

ISBN: 978-0-9981096-4-0
Library of Congress Control Number: 2021925168

Printed in the United States of America
26 25 24 23 22/10 9 8 7 6 5 4 3 2 1

"Thanks be to God, who gives us the victory through our Lord Jesus Christ."

1ˢᵗ Corinthians 15:57

✝ TABLE OF CONTENTS ✝

INTRODUCTION: Defeeted!   11

BOOK ONE
1   The Scriptures as Our Guide   15
2   Facing Your Philistine   21
3   Your Adversary   25
4   Deciding to Resist   29
5   Cutting Off the Water Supply   33
6   Rebuilding Your Walls   43
7   On the Alert   53
8   Weapons for War   63
9   Standing on God's Promises   83
10 Overcoming Discouragement   93
11 Pray, Pray, Pray!   97

BOOK TWO
1   Unforgiven!   115
2   Our Forgiving God   117
3   The Cross: the Basis of Our Forgiveness   121
4   King David Forgiven   125
5   Sexual Sin Forgiven   133
6   The High Cost of Forgiveness   139
7   The Slain Lamb of God   143
8   Amazing Grace   149
9   Examples of Forgiveness   161
10 Seventy Times Seven   167
11 A Root of Bitterness   173
12 Letting Go   181
13 Father, Forgive Them   187

BOOK ONE

✝ INTRODUCTION ✝
Defeeted

There's no doubt in my mind that some eagle-eyed grammatical guru has concluded "defeeted" is spelt incorrectly. Yes, you are right. However, the mistake was intentional, not accidental.

Let me explain.

Throughout the Word of God, *the feet* are invariably associated with dominion, authority, victory, etc. Paul (writing to the Romans) states:

> "The God of peace will soon crush Satan under your feet."
>
> Romans 16:20

I could list numerous scriptures to support this fact. *Defeeted* is my way of saying that far too many Christians have had their feet cut out from under them—leaving them in a "defeeted" state.

They no longer know how to put their foot down and claim the victory that is theirs in Christ Jesus. Consequently, they run from counsellor to counsellor in the hope of finding someone to slay their giants for them (more about that later).

I believe God wants to open your eyes to the fact that He has given you your feet not only so you can stand physically but also spiritually and victoriously!

†

In the Book of Revelation, Jesus exhorts us (over and over again) to be *overcomers*. This is not only for our own spiritual well-being now but ultimately for His eternal purposes. God is preparing *a bride* for His Son. Most of us find it hard to believe—but this will be our eternal role: *the wife of The Lamb*.

When we read about marriage in the New Testament, the first requirement is that we not be "unequally yoked." Most of us understand that this refers to the fact that (as believers) we should not marry someone who is an unbeliever. That being said, I also believe we can be unequally yoked with another believer. Take, for instance, a person who has a clear calling for missionary work but marries someone who has no interest in missions whatsoever.

When we think of our eternal calling, as the wife of the Lamb, we need to consider exactly who we are going to be yoked to and for what purpose. The younger generation of believers think of marriage from a more secular and sensual viewpoint. Their minds may be more occupied with the bedroom than the throne room; they may be inclined to think of romance, rather than ruling.

The fact is we are going to be united in marriage to a king. Not merely an ordinary king but the King of all kings. How then will we fulfill our role as helpmate, if we are unable to overcome our own problems and affairs?

Our earthly battles are God's way of preparing us to reign with Him.

†

We read in the Book of Revelation that the Bride is likened to a city coming down to earth out of heaven. The gates that permit access into the city are all made of the same substance—*pearl*. Why not bronze, iron, brass, silver, or gold? Why is each gate formed of a single pearl? Because pearls are formed by problems.

The following information explains with more detail:

> "A natural pearl forms when an irritant works its way into a particular species of oyster, mussel, or clam. As a defense mechanism, the mollusk secretes a fluid to coat the irritant. Layer upon layer of this coating is deposited on the irritant until a lustrous pearl is formed." *("How Pearls Are Formed," J. Thomas Jewelers)*

In like manner, the Lord allows us to face various trials and difficulties so that we too can, by the grace of God, turn our problems into pearls. We are about to embark on a journey and learn how to overcome. Welcome aboard!

✝ ONE ✝
The Scriptures as Our Guide

Most of our study will be based on the life of one of Israel's great kings. His name is Hezekiah. Now, before you decide to toss this book aside thinking, *What lessons can I learn from a king who died over two thousand years ago?* allow me to explain. The Apostle Paul reminds us:

> "For whatever was written in earlier times was written for our instruction, that through perseverance and the encouragement of the Scriptures we might have hope." Romans 15:4

Paul likewise reminded Timothy:

"All Scripture is inspired by God and is profitable for teaching, for reproof, for correction, for training in righteousness that the man of God may be adequately equipped for every good work." 2 Timothy 3:16-17

When Paul writes to the Corinthian believers, he reminds them of Israel's failure to enter into the Promised Land:

"Now these things happened to them as an example and they were written for our instruction upon whom the ends of the ages has come."
1 Corinthians 10:11

When holy men of God wrote what is now known as the Bible, they wrote as moved upon by the Holy Spirit. We need to understand that God's Word is not just thrown together randomly, but it's meticulously pieced together by the Holy Spirit for our spiritual profit.

Now that we have a biblical basis for our study, we are going to be looking at the thirty second chapter of Second Chronicles. This chapter is rich in spiritual wealth for those taking the time to meditate on it. Someone once described meditation as being similar to a cow chewing its cud. The cow begins by grazing as much grass as it can. It then settles down and begins to regurgitate what it has eaten, and then it slowly chews and chews until every bit of grass is broken down by the saliva it secretes, thereby acquiring all the nutrients possible from the grass.

Many of us read God's Word, but we fail to really extract any value from it because we read it too hastily. We need to read each verse over and over again, allowing the Holy Spirit to speak and apply it to our lives. This is what true meditation is all about. Here is how the famous Martin Luther taught his children to read God's Word:

"I study my Bible as I gather apples. First, I shake the whole tree that the ripest might fall. Then I shake each limb, and when I have shaken each limb, I shake each branch and every twig. Then I look under every leaf.

"I search the Bible as a whole, like shaking the whole tree. Then I shake every limb—study book after book. Then I shake every branch, giving attention to the chapters when they do not break the sense. Then I shake every twig, or a careful study of the paragraphs and sentences and words and their meanings."

Another author says the best way to read the Bible is to read each chapter and then go back and quarter inch your way through it. In other words, take your time to ponder each and every word.

Let's get started.

THE ENEMY SHOWS UP

The last two verses of 2 Chronicles 31 provide us with a great summary of king Hezekiah's life. I've told my wife on several occasions that if I die before she does, I would be honored to have these two verses on my tombstone (with the obvious modifications; my name instead of his etc.):

> "And thus Hezekiah did throughout all of Judah, and he did what was good, right, and true before the Lord his God. And every work that he began in the service of the house of God in law and in commandment, seeking his God, he did with all his heart and prospered."
> 2 Chronicles 31:20-21

Unfortunately, the chapter ends there. But if you keep reading, it goes on to state:

> "After these acts of faithfulness Sennacherib king of Assyria came . . ."

In other words, the enemy showed up. Notice it wasn't after acts of rebellion, perversion, sin, disobedience, or anger, etc. After Hezekiah was faithful to God, the enemy came to harass him!

I remind fellow believers all the time that a good indication that you are prospering spiritually is if the enemy is constantly harassing you. In fact, if the enemy is *not* harassing you, you should ask yourself why. *Why am I of no threat to the enemy?*

Let's face it, there are numerous nations that America doesn't need to worry about. Take Tahiti for example. This little island nation in the South Pacific has no nuclear power, no real military might, and therefore it poses no threat to America. Russia and China, on the other hand, are two nations we keep close tabs on because they have the means to destroy us.

To Hezekiah, Assyria was the equivalent of *Russia and China* combined. Assyria was the superpower of her day. Sennacherib and his vast army had already conquered nation after nation, and now they were heading toward Jerusalem.

If you were Hezekiah, what would you do? Stay tuned.

† TWO †
Facing Your Philistine

Before we delve into this chapter, it's important to understand the necessity for war. I'm not referring to war in the *natural* but in the realm of the *spirit*. To explain, allow me to recount God's dealings with Israel as they came out of Egypt—and later His *about face* concerning the very same people.

When God delivered His people from Egypt's reign of terror, He parted the Red Sea in order to bring them to the wilderness—and eventually into the Promised Land. God foresaw that the most direct route would take His people directly through the territory of the Philistines, so He chose another route.

"Now it came about when Pharaoh had let the people go, that God did not lead them by way of the land of the Philistines, even though it was near; for God said, 'Lest the people change their minds when they see war, and they return to Egypt.' Hence God led the people around by the way of the wilderness." Exodus 13:17-18

God is a responsible Father; He looked at the spiritual condition of His people and saw them as mere children. They were *babes in Christ,* so to speak. They had only just been redeemed by the blood of the lamb and were by no means ready to fight. God understood this, so He took His people on a longer (but safer) route, thereby protecting them from war.

A TIME FOR WAR

Now let's jump ahead to the time of the Judges. Israel had finally entered the Promised Land. It not only flowed with milk and honey but also with giants. Consider what the Lord did:

"Now these are the nations that the Lord left to test Israel by them (that is all who had not experienced any of the wars of Canaan; only in order that the generations of the sons of Israel might be taught war, those who had not experienced formerly). These nations are: the five lords of the Philistines . . ."
Judges 3:1-3

Here we see the Lord leaving the Philistines in the land in order for Israel to be taught war. This is an essential lesson for every believer to learn! There's a time when God will take you around a problem because you are not spiritually able to deal with it. But eventually the time will come when He makes you face your enemy. He wants to teach you how to wage war.

I well recall our oldest daughter coming home from school one day. We were involved in missionary work in Papua New Guinea at the time, and our daughter attended an Australian Army base school. Her teacher had assigned some math problems as her homework. Our daughter wanted me to help her; a task I could have completed in a matter of seconds. Instead, I made her solve the problems herself. Today she has a Master's degree. If I had stepped in and done her homework for her, I would have created an ongoing problem for myself, but I also would have stunted my daughter's mental development.

There were times during my years of pastoral ministry when I refused to pray for one of my people. I wasn't trying to be unkind, but knowing them as I did, I knew it was time for them to begin slaying their own giants! We do a tremendous disservice to our people by always praying for every "owie" they get. We do have a role to play in helping others. But there's a fine line between helping and hindering growth. My late father once said, "If there had been a soup kitchen at the prodigal's pig-pen, he would have never returned to his father's house!"

GROWING UP

The apostle John, in his first epistle, writes about three levels of spiritual maturity. He addresses the children, the young men, and the fathers. The *children* he refers to as having *had their sins forgiven*. But the "young men" he says are strong, having the Word of God abiding in them and having overcome the evil one.

Children are totally dependent on someone else to protect them and take care of their needs. Overcoming the evil one, on the other hand, is a sign of maturity.

In the following chapter we will return to the story of Hezekiah and the steps he took in overcoming his enemy, King Sennacherib.

✝ THREE ✝
Your Adversary

Hezekiah ascended the throne after the death of his father Ahaz, who just happened to be one of the most wicked kings of Israel. Ahaz had closed the doors of the temple and led the nation into paganism during his reign.

After the death of Ahaz, Hezekiah became king at the age of twenty-five. His first official act was to cleanse the temple and turn the nation back to God. Hezekiah brought about one of the great Old Testament revivals. Then, in Chapter 32, Hezekiah faced his greatest test of faith, wisdom, and courage. Like David of old, he met his own giant—Sennacherib's terrifying army.

RECOGNIZING YOUR ENEMY

As we consider the details of this chapter, bear in mind that the Holy Spirit recorded them for our instruction and training. God often uses the natural to reveal the spiritual. I trust that will become evident as you allow the Holy Spirit to open your understanding and help you apply these lessons to your own circumstances, whatever they may be.

The very first thing that Hezekiah became aware of was that he had an enemy:

> "When Hezekiah saw that Sennacherib had come and that he intended to make war on Jerusalem . . ." 2 Chronicles 32:2

As believers, we also must realize that we have an enemy who is at war with us. Far too many believers dismiss this fact. The Word of God refers to Satan as *your* adversary the devil. He is a formidable foe; he has brought millions into bondage under his diabolical and deceptive ways. We read in the book of Jude that even Michael the archangel respected the devil's authority.

The devil first appears in the opening chapters of Genesis where he deceived Eve; he continues to show up all the way through the Bible to the book of Revelation. His trophies and achievements are legendary. His goal is to set up his own kingdom while seeking to destroy the Kingdom of God. Therefore, any sincere believer is going to be targeted by his demonic agents.

Paul warned the Corinthians: "Don't be ignorant concerning the devil's schemes or ways!" And yet many people have opened themselves to the enemy without even being aware of it. I don't believe every problem is a result of some demonic activity but neither should we dismiss this possibility.

RECOGNIZE YOUR ENEMY'S TOOLS

Prior to their conversion, scores of believers played with Ouija-boards or dabbled in other forms of witchcraft. This type of activity can have lingering or lasting effects. However, while I don't intend to delve into every type of demonic activity, we do need to recognize that these are not the only tools in the devil's toolbox. We're warned numerous times in God's Word that the devil is actively trying to deceive us. Jesus made it clear that *deception* would be a growing problem prior to His return. Much of the deception Jesus mentioned had to do with the spiritual realm, including signs and wonders. Hopefully you understand that *your* adversary, the devil, is prowling around seeking to take whatever advantage he can to ensnare you and enslave you. Remember, the enemy comes to steal kill and destroy. His goal is your destruction.

I vividly recall hearing my beloved pastor, mentor, and fellow elder Peter Morrow telling the story of the devil "tidying up his workshop." The demons that were helping him would hold up various objects, and the devil would then decide if they were of any value to him or not.

One demon, upon finding an old, very worn-out item, held it up thinking, *This looks like it has served its purposes.*

The devil immediately responded, saying, "No, no! Don't throw that away; it's one of my most successful tools!"

"But what is it?" the demon asked.

"Discouragement!" the devil replied.

Hezekiah had to first *recognize* his enemy before he could take the necessary steps to *defeat* him. We must do the same.

✝ FOUR ✝

Deciding to Resist

Once Hezekiah recognized that he was under the threat of war (verse 3) he immediately decided to resist. Far too often we fail to take whatever steps necessary to resist our adversary the devil. It's one thing to acknowledge the devil's existence, but it's an entirely different matter to make a conscious decision to do something about it.

Just having theological knowledge is not sufficient. He is your foe! He's determined to destroy you by whatever means he can. Most believers have read Paul's letter to the Ephesians, where he talks about putting on the whole armor of God. But how many of us really take this seriously? "Out of sight, out of mind" describes the attitude of many.

But on the other hand, some give the devil too much credit! My father often told the story of the devil sitting by the side of the road sobbing.

A well-meaning believer approached him and asked, "Why are you sobbing?"

The devil responded, "Because of you believers who blame me for all the things I'd love to do but don't have the time to do!" Blaming the devil for everything is a mistake—but so is ignoring him completely.

WAKE UP!

On the evening of September 10th, 2001, my wife drove me to the Dallas Fort Worth Airport to catch a flight to Korea, and then on to Malaysia. I boarded the flight around 2 am the morning of September the 11th.

Once on board, we settled down for a twelve-hour flight to Seoul. The cabin lights were dimmed, and my fellow passengers made themselves comfortable and attempted to sleep. Four or five hours passed before we were suddenly awakened by the captain announcing that we were returning to the United States. We would be landing in Anchorage, Alaska in forty-five minutes. I don't recall his exact words, but he informed us that there had been some type of incident—and all flights were being forced to land.

Since we were virtually outside of the continental United States, we were one of the last planes to land. The airport looked like a massive parking lot of planes as we landed and taxied to the gate. After being shuttled through the airport, we boarded buses and were driven to Seward, Alaska—because all of the hotels in Anchorage were already filled with passengers from other flights!

We soon learned more details. Once settled in our hotel, we turned the television on, joining the rest of the nation who was watching (over and over again) the planes flying into the Twin Towers, etc. There's more to that story, but the point I am trying to make is that, prior to that day, America considered herself almost invincible. It was a watershed moment for America.

CHANGING PERSPECTIVES

Since that day, we have become much more security conscious as a nation. Now it's impossible to fly anywhere without going through some type of detector or security check.

Just as 9-11 became a wake-up call for America, we believers need a spiritual wake up of our own! The devil is on the warpath, and unless we take his power seriously, and then decide to act, we will join the devil's long list of trophies.

After recognizing his enemy and making a decision to resist, Hezekiah began the necessary steps to overcome his enemy. His actions are an example that we must follow.

† FIVE †

Cutting Off the Water Supply

Hezekiah's first act of resistance, after making his decision to fight, was to cut off any source of water around Jerusalem. Water was essential to sustain life. If the enemy came and found water... Well, go ahead and read it for yourself:

> "He decided with his officers and warriors to cut off the supply of water from the springs which were outside the city, and they helped him. So many people assembled and stopped up all the springs and the stream which flowed through the region, saying, 'Why should the kings of Assyria come and find abundant water?'" (verses 3-4)

In essence what Hezekiah was doing was to remove anything that could sustain the life of his enemy. If the Assyrians arrived and found an abundance of water, then they could set up their camp and stay indefinitely. Hezekiah and his people would eventually be forced to surrender, or starve to death within the city walls.

YOUR ENEMY'S BASIC NEEDS

Removing the water supply was an old and effective means of ridding yourself of your opponent. In fact, during the days of Abraham, the Philistines filled in his wells—effectively forcing him to leave the area. Recognizing that your enemies have basic needs— and that you've been supplying them—is the first step to freedom and victory.

As we saw, Hezekiah decided to not only acknowledge that he had an enemy but also to fight or resist that enemy. In the body of Christ, many have decided to fight—but there's been a tendency to attempt resistance by simply saying something like, "I rebuke you Satan!" Resistance implies much more than just quoting a few phrases. Paul uses the word *wrestle* when dealing with our enemy. I know a little about wrestling, having made the "A" squad in high school (when I was sixty years younger and fifty pounds lighter). I wish that all I had to do was utter a few words and then watch as my opponent flew onto his back, glued to the ground! But, of course, wrestling (like all resisting) involves pitting your strength against the strength of your opponent—until one of you gains the advantage and wins the battle.

SHAKING OFF THE ENEMY'S FOOTHOLD

Let's go back to verses 3 and 4. I want you to notice exactly *what* Hezekiah did. He had to stop up the springs, as well as stop up a stream. These were not just puddles of water that could be filled in with a load of sand or soil. A spring has force behind it, as does a flowing stream. This was an extremely difficult task, requiring hours (if not days) of work. This same determination must be applied by those seeking freedom from whatever spiritual attack they are under, whether it be fear or failure.

Cutting off the water can be compared to *repentance*. Sin, in whatever form, allows the enemy a foothold, or stronghold, in our lives. Paul warned the Ephesians with these words:

> "Do not give the devil an opportunity." Ephesians 4:27. *(The literal translation reads: "Do not give the devil a place.")*

When we engage in sin, we give the enemy legal grounds to establish strongholds in our lives. Repentance removes those landing strips, so to speak.

Jesus made it clear to His disciples that they were to preach a message of repentance in order for forgiveness to take place. And He said to them:

> "Thus it is written, that the Christ should suffer and rise again from the dead the third day; and that repentance for forgiveness of sins should be proclaimed in His name to all nations beginning from Jerusalem . . ." Luke 24:46-47

Just as Hezekiah had to search the terrain around Jerusalem to identify the locations of the various springs that could sustain his enemy, so we too need to allow the Holy Spirit to search our hearts. You recall King David's cry for God to search his heart:

> "Search me O God, and know my heart; Try me, and know my thoughts: And see if there be any wicked way in me." Psalm 132:23-24

THE HOLY SPIRIT'S ROLE

Repentance need not be some long, drawn-out process whereby we exhaust ourselves trying to ferret out every conceivable sin we have ever committed. Neither should it be just superficial or a casual glance over our life. Repentance is something we need the Spirit of God for; one of the main tasks of the Holy Spirit is to convict us of sin.

He reveals, and we respond.

Just a few weeks after being married, my wife and I drove out to Brooklyn, New York to work with Teen Challenge under the leadership of David Wilkerson.

In one of the very first messages I heard Brother David speak, he shared how, during the early days of his ministry, he spent time each evening with the Lord, in study and prayer. He had formed a habit of analyzing the way he had spent his day. Invariably he found himself mired in condemnation as he recalled all the missed opportunities, etc. After days or weeks of feeling totally defeated, he heard the Holy Spirit speak to him, asking why he had assumed the role of the Holy Spirit. The Lord revealed to him that it was not his job, but it was the role of the Holy Spirit to convict of sin.

Take time to allow the Holy Spirit to bring to your remembrance any areas of your life that you have never really acknowledged and repented of. This may happen over a period of time, as we have a tendency to sweep some things under the rug without really repenting and turning from them.

COMING CLEAN

During The Welsh Revival, God anointed a young man by the name of Evan Roberts as one of His main instruments in transforming Wales. Allow me to quote from the book titled *Rent Heavens:*

> "Mr. Roberts himself gradually ceased to speak at his own meetings... At the first he spoke pointedly, and often at much length. Sometimes he would speak for close to an hour before setting the meeting open for praise and prayer. And what he did say was most valuable.
>
> Everywhere he would set before the people what became known as 'The Four Points.' Did they desire an outpouring of the Spirit? Very well; four conditions must be observed. And, they are essential.
>
> * Is there any sin in your past that you have not confessed to God? On your knees at once. Your past must be put away, and yourself cleansed.
>
> * Is there anything in your life that is doubtful—anything that you cannot decide whether it is good or evil? Away with it. There must be no cloud between you and God.
>
> Have you forgiven everybody, everybody, EVERYBODY? If not, don't expect forgiveness for your own sins. *(We will deal with the area of unforgiveness in a later chapter.)*

* Do what the Spirit prompts you to do. Obedience, prompt, implicit, unquestionable obedience to the Spirit.

*A public confession of Christ as your Savior. there's a vast difference between profession and confession."

One of the great tactics of the enemy is to convince you that you are too filthy or defiled to ever be set free. In other words, you have crossed the line and are now beyond redemption. Nothing could be further from the truth. The blood of Jesus Christ cleanses from *all* sin. Some of the most prevalent sins are the sins of the flesh—especially sexual sin. These sins are often covered or hidden and seldom spoken about from the pulpit. The enemy, however, delights in using them to hold us in bondage—telling us there is no way of escape. Statistically, the vast majority of professing Christians have some degree of addiction to pornography. This certainly becomes fertile ground for the enemy. Someone reading this is crying out, "Is there any hope for me?" Allow me to share some great news with you. Remember that in a previous chapter I quoted the Apostle Paul's letter to the Romans in which he wrote:

"Whatever was written in earlier times was written for our instruction, that through perseverance and the encouragement of the Scriptures we might have hope." Romans 15:4

In Paul's letter to the Corinthians, he shares some amazing truths concerning God's miraculous power to cleanse and transform one's life and lifestyle. My father would often remind his listeners that to refer to someone as a 'Corinthian' was equal to calling them all the vile and profane language you could think of but summed up in one word. Corinth was vile in every way. When Paul wrote to the church in Corinth, he reminds them of their past:

"Do not be deceived; neither fornicators, nor idolaters, nor adulterers, nor effeminate, nor homosexuals, nor thieves, nor covetous, nor drunkards, nor revilers, nor swindlers, shall inherit the kingdom of God.

And such were some of you, but you were washed, but you were sanctified, but you were justified in the name of the Lord Jesus Christ, and in the Spirit of our God." 1 Corinthians 6:11-12

Now if that isn't good enough for you to get excited about, then what I'm about to share next will. We have tens of thousands, or even millions, of believers that have been guilty of sexual sin prior to marriage. In other words, they have lost their virginity and live with that regret. Now comes the greatest news of all: in Paul's second letter to the Corinthians, he reminds them:

"For I am jealous for you with a godly jealousy; for I betrothed you to one husband, that to Christ I might present you a pure virgin."
2 Corinthians 11:2

Wow! What do you think of that? Only the blood of Jesus can restore your virginity. God no longer sees you as just forgiven but restored. Hallelujah! We have more ground to cover, so we must move on.

† SIX †
Rebuilding Your Walls

Returning to the account of Hezekiah and the steps he took to overcome his enemy Sennacherib, let's now focus on another vital step: *rebuilding the walls*.

We read in verse 5:

"And he took courage and rebuilt all the walls that had been broken down . . ."

Walls have always been, and will remain, a necessary means of security—whether for your home, business, or even nation. We still have numerous cities throughout Europe with walls. Some, to be sure, are a mere reminder of their previous grandeur—

having been allowed to crumble or fall. During their time, they served to protect and provide peace to those sheltering or living within them. Jerusalem was no exception. Long periods of peace, however, can also allow the walls to become neglected and fall into disrepair.

Now in case you are asking yourself, "What do walls have to do with me?" let me explain: The writer of *Proverbs* reminds us that we, as individuals, are like a city surrounded by a wall. Listen to what he says:

> "Like a city that is broken into and without walls is a man who has no control over his spirit."
> Proverbs 25:28

In contrast to this verse, consider what the Lord said to the prophet Jeremiah:

> "'Behold, I have made you today as a fortified city, and as a pillar of iron and as walls of bronze against the whole land, to the kings of Judah, to its princes, to its priests and to the people of the land. And they will fight against you, but they will not overcome you, for I am with you to deliver you,' declares the Lord." Jeremiah 1:18-19

When a city has well-built and fortified walls, its residents are secure, knowing that their city is impenetrable. When a city's walls begin to fall into disrepair, it becomes vulnerable to attack. Hezekiah was well aware of this, and so he began rebuilding the area of wall that had been broken down.

AREAS OF WEAKNESS

Whether it was Hezekiah or one of his men, they had to examine each area of the city's wall to determine where they were most vulnerable. In other words, they took the time to identify their areas of weakness. We all have areas of weakness that make us susceptible to the enemy's attack.

According to the writer of Hebrews we are all prone to *besetting sins*. Have you ever wondered why the enemy always seems to attack you with the same thoughts or temptations? That's not because he is omniscient and knows everything about you—only God knows that. But the devil is clever. I like to compare the enemy to a skilled fisherman.

Every man who loves to fish not only owns a rod and reel but also a tackle box. The tackle box holds all of the necessary tools, including an assortment of hooks and lures. Once the fisherman finds the best lure for his prey, he inevitably leaves it on the line because it is doing its job. If he begins fishing in a new location, he may try several lures until he finds the best one for that particular lake or river. Likewise, your enemy is a crafty fisherman; he figured out your areas of vulnerability long ago. Because he has determined your weaknesses, he will continue to fish away—until you rebuild the areas of your life that are prone to attack.

REBUILDING MEANS REPLACING

Just as cutting off the water supply requires effort and time, rebuilding the wall of your life doesn't happen overnight. Once you have honestly identified your areas of weakness or vulnerability, it's time to rebuild. But rebuilding is not usually about propping up what has fallen; it requires replacing the old with newer and better materials. The Apostle Paul gives us some poignant points in this regard:

> "Let him that steals steal no longer, but rather let him labor, performing with his own hands what is good, in order that he may have something to share with him who has need. Let no unwholesome word proceed from your mouth, but only such a word as is good for edification according to the need of the moment, that it may give grace to those who hear. And do not grieve the Holy Spirit of God, by whom you were sealed for the day of redemption. Let all bitterness and wrath and anger and clamor and slander be put away from you, along with all malice. And be kind to one another, tender hearted, for-

giving each another, just as God in Christ has forgiven you." Ephesians 4:28-32

Here we see Paul addressing three problems. I doubt that Paul has just one individual in mind, although that is possible. I'd rather think he's referring to three major problems that he saw in the church body. The first being theft, the second gossip, and the third unforgiveness. Let's look at these areas of weakness (sin) and see how Paul admonishes those involved: the first thing Paul does is *identify the problem* or sin. He says to those who are guilty of theft, "Stop!" But that doesn't do anything to eliminate the problem. We rebuild the wall by doing the opposite of what we were doing before. Instead of stealing, Paul tells them to find employment. "Let him labor." Not only should they find a job, for their own sakes, but they should begin to look for ways to meet the needs of others!

When my wife and I began working with Brother David Wilkerson, I was invited by one of the staff to become involved in a prison ministry. Every week we would catch the subway and then take the ferry to Riker's Island. If I recall, there were several thousand inmates there charged and convicted of theft. The reason was *heroin addiction*.

The average heroin addict needed to support a "$60.00 to $200.00 a day" habit. In order to meet that need, he would have to steal hundreds of dollars' worth of merchandise each day. You can imagine the suffering and disappointment of people coming home from a hard day's work only to find their valuable possessions stolen. If you multiply that by several thousand you can begin to calculate not only the financial loss but also the emotional toll caused by these addicts. Keep in mind that those incarcerated were only a fraction of the number compared to the multiple thousands still roaming the various suburbs of New York.

No doubt Paul was thinking of the sorrow and disappointment thieves inflict upon innocent victims, perhaps even some in his own flock. Paul told those who were guilty of theft to work hard and learn to meet the needs of others. In other words, instead of thinking about themselves, they were encouraged to consider how they could meet the needs of others.

The second problem Paul mentioned was gossip or destructive talk. He used the term *unwholesome*, referring to those whose mission in life is to demean and tear down others reputations. Once again, he urged those involved to stop—*let no unwholesome word proceed out of your mouth*. But that was only the first step. Paul insisted that they begin to speak good and *edifying* words. Start building people up by extending them grace when you refer to them. This is taking the opposite approach to what they had been involved in.

Finally, Paul spoke about those harboring bitterness, unforgiveness, anger, etc. His solution: *forgive!* (We will discuss unforgiveness later.)

FRUITS OF PERSISTENCE

Bad habits are not formed in an instant. Likewise, any habit you've developed will not usually disappear overnight. (Although all things are possible with God!) Throughout the New Testament we are exhorted to grow, run, put on, strive, work, fight, and wrestle, etc. All of these require determination, effort, and time.

Back in my Bible School days I battled with lustful thoughts. My mind was like an open sewer, and yet I was in training for the ministry! My mornings were spent listening to men of God teach, as well as attending the weekly chapel services. My afternoons were spent in the graphics department of their publication department. It was here that my enemy seemed to have a field day. My mind was constantly barraged with every temptation imaginable. Needless to say, I felt ashamed. How could I ever witness of the transforming power of God, when I was a captive myself?!

And then one day, I made a conscious decision. Instead of cowering in hopelessness, I decided to wage war on the enemy. My city was under attack, and my walls were broken down. But I determined to fight!

That first day, I must have rebuked the devil a thousand times. The second day nine hundred. After a solid month I had won the battle. Now, by the grace of God, the moment a thought assails me I find myself declaring, "Satan, the Lord rebuke you!"

Now please don't misunderstand me, I'm not claiming the victory was achieved by my own will power alone. But neither did I expect to achieve victory by prayer alone. Paul made clear to the Ephesians that we have to play *our role* in the conflict. A good way to illustrate this point is to remind you of Moses and Joshua. Following their deliverance from Egypt they were attacked by the Amalekites. Moses commissioned Joshua to gather together the men and prepare to fight. While the sons of Israel were fighting, Moses (along with Aaron and Hur) positioned himself on the top of the hill overlooking the battle. Moses raised his hands toward heaven, while Joshua and his men engaged the enemy.

As long as Moses had his hands raised to heaven, Israel prevailed. However, as the battle continued, Moses became tired. He could no longer keep his hands raised. Tragically, the moment Moses lowered his hands, the battle changed in favor of the Amalekites. But Aaron and Hur immediately took their stand alongside Moses and raised his hands, thereby allowing the men of Israel to win the battle.

It took working together to win—one without the other wasn't enough. And the battle required dogged persistence; it would have been lost if they had taken their ease.

We will look at this again soon.

✝ SEVEN ✝
On the Alert

Following the rebuilding of the walls, Hezekiah went about erecting towers on the wall. While we are not told how many towers were erected, we know there were more than one.

The purpose of the towers was to provide the watchmen an unobstructed view of the land around the city and beyond. The watchmen had the responsibility of discerning if a cloud of dust that they saw was an approaching army, a caravan of merchants wanting to sell their goods, or just the wind stirring up the distant dust. If they determined that they were in trouble, they would sound the alarm by blowing the ram's horn. Once the horn was blown, other watchmen would join them, signaling to the people in the fields outside that they were facing the possible threat of danger. Those outside the city walls would gather or round up anything needed to sustain life and then head for safety within the walls.

Watchtowers were a primitive, yet effective, means of saving lives, not to mention the city.

ARMING YOUR SECURITY SYSTEM

Today we have far more sophisticated means of protecting ourselves. The security business is a multi-billion dollar a year industry—offering home protection, fire protection, identity protection, computer protection, plus a host of others—including national security, etc. However, many believers fail to install any spiritual protection. They spend fortunes guarding their belongings, yet fail to guard their most precious possession: their soul.

God's Word warns us to be vigilant concerning our enemy, the devil. He's a far greater threat than any other thief, and he's constantly looking for ways to destroy, deceive, discourage, or devour us.

Jesus, following His time of testing in the wilderness, continued to face the devil's sinister attacks. We read:

"And when the devil had finished every temptation, he departed from him until a more opportune time." Luke 4:13

We never know when the enemy is going to pounce. He waits for those opportune times; for that reason, we need to be constantly on the alert. When we let our guard down, then we become the target of the enemy's fiery darts. Make no mistake about, it we are not fighting against flesh and blood, although the enemy may use people for his purposes. We are up against a formidable foe with thousands of years of experience.

SECURING YOUR MIND

There are practical things we can do to ward off the enemy's attack. My first suggestion is that you keep your mind occupied. We've all heard the saying: "An idle mind is the devil's workshop."

I recall listening to one of my early mentors, a gentleman by the name of Neville Winger. We were living in New Zealand at the time, on the Great Barrier Island. Neville was an unassuming but wise and godly man who owned and directed the community living there. In one of his messages, he referenced King David and what led up to his infamous sin with Bathsheba. Following his sin, David was confronted by the prophet Nathan who told David a story about a poor man who had nothing but a little ewe lamb. The prophet's story summarized what the king had done. Neville explained all of this, and then read: "Now a traveler came to the rich man." (2 Samuel 12:4) Here Neville paused to say, "Watch out for travelers!" The rich man's sin against his neighbor began innocently enough, by simply allowing a traveler to enter his home. As Neville explained, it became clear that he was likening the *traveler* to a *thought*.

Over the years since, I've often pondered those words. *Now a traveler came* . . . Temptation begins with a thought.

Travelers will come. What we do with them will ultimately determine our destiny. Remember the saying of Emerson:

> Sow a thought, reap and act;
> Sow and act and you reap a habit;
> Sow a habit and you reap a character;
> Sow a character, and you reap a destiny.

Little wonder then that Paul, writing to the believers in Rome, exhorts his readers:

> . . . "be transformed by the renewing of your mind." Romans 12:2

Let me phrase that a little differently: renewing your mind will transform you. We read in the Book of Proverbs:

"As a man thinks in his heart, so is he."

A HIGHER MIND SET

Writing to the Philippians, Paul reminds them:

"Finally, brothers, whatever is true, whatever is honorable, whatever is right, whatever is pure, whatever is lovely, whatever is commendable, if there is any excellence and if anything worthy of praise, think about these things." Philippians 4:8

When a vessel is full, there's no room left for anything else. Not only is this true of a container but also our mind. If we can learn to keep our minds preoccupied, then the enemy has little ground to work with. There are several ways to do this. Paul exhorted the Colossian believers with the following:

"If then you have been raised up with Christ, keep seeking the things above, where Christ is seated at the right hand of God. Set your mind on the things above, not on the things that are on earth . . ."
Colossians 3:1-2

We often refer to someone as having a certain *mind set*, meaning it's almost impossible to persuade them to change their way of thinking. That can be either a positive or negative attitude, depending on what they set their mind on.

If we learn to set our mind on Christ, there's little room left for the enemy to fill it. As Paul continues in this same chapter of Colossians:

"Let the word of Christ richly dwell within you, with all wisdom teaching and admonishing one another with psalms, and hymns and spiritual songs, singing with thankfulness in your hearts to God." Colossians 3:16

This then is another way of transforming your mind: *fill it with the Word of God and song.*

THE BATTLE FOR YOUR HEART

Incidentally, when the Scriptures refer to the heart this doesn't usually mean the organ that circulates the blood. We discover something very interesting when we read the first three times the word *heart* is mentioned in Genesis. The first mention is in Genesis 6:5, where it refers to the "thoughts of his heart." The second time says that the Lord "was grieved in His heart." The third mention of *heart* is in Chapter Eight;

after the flood, we read in verse twenty-one: ... "and the Lord said to Himself, 'I will never again curse the ground ...'" The literal rendering reads: ... "and the Lord said in His heart, 'I will never again curse the ground ...'" He said this *in His heart!*

From these first three mentions of the word, we gain the following understanding: *the heart* refers to:

The mind, the emotions, and the will.

Therefore, it's no surprise that these three are the major battlegrounds of your enemy. When God says, "Son, give me your heart," (Proverbs 23:26) God is asking you to yield your mind, will, and emotions to Him. In Psalm 86:11 David prayed:

"Unite my heart to fear thy name."

A divided heart is one where the mind is convinced about something but the emotions are reluctant to follow.

Take, for instance, a person addicted to tobacco. His physician shows him the damage that tobacco can do to his lungs. He is convinced *in his mind* that the physician is correct, but *his emotions* tell him a different story. He loves tobacco! His mind and his emotions do not agree, so he has an undivided heart.

This poor man's heart will remain divided until he *wills* to make a change. His *will* can override his mind and emotions, thereby uniting his heart. The *will* is a mighty force. Willpower is given to us by God, enabling us to make godly decisions.

FEARING GOD = HATING EVIL

Another key to defeat the enemy's schemes is to ask God for godly fear or *the fear of the Lord.*

During my high school years, I was subject to every imaginable temptation. While drugs were not a problem in those days, sexual promiscuity, alcohol, theft, and other forms of trouble-making were.

Whenever I faced one of those temptations, I immediately thought of my father—and of his reaction if he were to find out! I loved my father deeply, and I knew it would break his heart if heard about it. That fear kept me out of trouble during my teenage years.

When I say that I *feared* my father, I'm not implying that I was afraid of him. I'm speaking of my deep love and respect for who he was and for the principles he lived by. The fear of God is no different. If we truly have the fear of God in our lives, we will not involve ourselves in things that grieve Him.

Fear is a natural deterrent. If you fear heights you are going to stay away from the edge of the cliffs. If you fear fire, you'll avoid getting near it. If we have the fear of God, the Bible says we will hate evil.

I wrote previously that my wife and I, along with our baby daughter, lived on the great Barrier Island in New Zealand for a season. Over the New Year we were privileged to attend the ministry's annual conference, which was held in a large tent, just a few hundred feet from the edge of Karaka Bay. The speakers that year included Loren Cunningham, founder of Youth with A Mission, Joy Dawson and Milton Smith.

One evening Milton spoke on "The fear of the Lord." Until that time, I don't recall ever hearing an entire message on *the fear of the Lord*. Following his message, I asked to speak with the various speakers, including the leader of the work—Neville Winger. We gathered in what was formerly an old whaling hut. I explained to the group that I knew it was wrong to sin, but I did not have a hatred for sin. I then asked them to lay hands on me and pray that I might know the fear of God in my life.

Over the years since, I've prayed that the Lord would increase the fear of God in my life. I'm convinced this is a vital and essential prayer for all who desire to live the life of an overcomer.

We are not through yet with how Hezekiah overcame his enemy. Let's continue.

✝ EIGHT ✝

Weapons for War

I trust you're beginning to see how the practical steps Hezekiah took to resist Sennacherib's advancing army have their spiritual counterpart in our lives.

No sooner had Hezekiah built the towers for the watchmen, than we read that he went about *making weapons and shields.*

All of his previous work, cutting off the water supply, rebuilding the crumbling walls, and erecting towers could be classified as *defensive action.* What Hezekiah did next was to take *offensive action.* He began to make and accumulate weapons to be used against the enemy.

GETTING TO KNOW YOUR WEAPONS

Thankfully, we don't need an arsenal of guns and ammo—our adversaries are spiritual. But we can learn from Hezekiah. Most notable is the order in which Hezekiah went about overcoming; it was not random but methodical. The same is true in our spiritual lives.

Our path to victory is not random but methodical—and has predictable results. While prayer is an important part of overcoming, prayer does not precede *repentance*. If we fail to "cut off" the ground that gave our enemy access, no amount of prayer will help.

Once we have cut off the water supply, rebuilt the walls, and erected towers, it's time to take *offensive action*. We must begin to use our weapons. We read:

> "For the weapons of our warfare are not of the flesh but divinely powerful for the destruction of fortresses." 2 Corinthians 10:4

We are at war, and our warfare is not physical but spiritual. However, God has not left us defenseless. As we read here, our weapons are powerful enough to destroy anything arrayed against us.

However, knowing that weapons exist does nothing for us. We must decide to *use* these weapons! Having several guns in your gun safe gives you no advantage if an intruder breaks into your house in the middle of the night. You must have your weapon close by and be ready to use it.

Similarly, many believers are aware of their adversary, but they have only a cursory knowledge of their God given weapons against him.

SUBMISSION

In Paul's letter to the Ephesians, we are instructed to *put on the full armor of God*. Many believers start here, and yet they fail to recognize the important truths and commands that precede this admonition, commands such as:

> "Your life must be controlled by love . . . Submit yourselves to one another because of your reverence for Christ . . ." Ephesians 5:2, 21

I strongly suggest that you take the time to study the latter part of Ephesians Chapter Five and the first nine verses of Chapter Six. In these verses Paul emphasizes the importance of *loving submission* to one another, out of reverence for Christ. He begins with submission in marriage, in the family, and finally in the workplace, etc. Incidentally, the opposite of *submission* is *rebellion*. Rebellion is what led to Lucifer's transformation from an anointed cherubim to a sinister serpent. The moment we allow rebellion in our own lives, we render ourselves powerless against the clever schemes of the devil.

Rebellion not only aligns us with the devil but also severs us from the very authority of God that we need to overcome our enemy. For example: how many times have you heard someone quote this?

> "Resist the devil and he will flee from you."
> James 4:7b

While this promise is certainly found in the book of James, many believers fail to quote *the entire verse*. Without the first part, the second becomes useless! The entire verse reads like this:

> "Submit therefore to God. Resist the devil and he will flee from you."

Our submission to God begins this process! We have little or no authority of our own—only as we acknowledge and submit to God's authority can we resist the devil. But if we harbor any rebellion toward God, it immediately renders us powerless in our spiritual resistance.

Rebellion can be linked to one very specific sickness or disease. In fact, it is the only sickness or disease that Jesus never healed. Do you know what sickness that was? When I tell you, I suspect you might argue and say I'm wrong. But the sickness I'm speaking of was *leprosy*.

Why do I say leprosy? If you'll recall, there were ten lepers, but only one returned to give thanks, etc. Yet the fact is, Jesus didn't *heal* any of them—He *cleansed* them!

Let me explain. When Jesus commissioned His disciples, he told them:

> "And as you go, preach saying, 'The kingdom of heaven is at hand.' Heal the sick, raise the dead, cleanse the lepers, cast out demons; freely you have received, freely give." Matthew 10:7-8

Notice that Jesus didn't tell His disciples to *heal* the lepers. Why didn't He include leprosy with every other sickness? Because leprosy had to be *cleansed*, not healed. The word that Jesus used here is the same word *cleanse* that's mentioned in John's epistle:

> "If we confess our sins, He is faithful and righteous to forgive us our sins and to cleanse us from all unrighteousness." 1 John 1:9

Many believers have been taught that leprosy is a *type* (or symbolic) of *sin*. But do you know which sin?

As you study leprosy, especially throughout the Old Testament, you'll come to an understanding that leprosy is almost always linked to *rebellion*. Rebellion is a sin and needs to be cleansed, not healed.

Let me illustrate this by taking you to several cases where the link between leprosy and rebellion is obvious: take the case of Miriam, the sister of Moses. She rebelled and spoke against the authority of Moses; she was immediately stricken with leprosy and had to be put out of the camp for seven days.

We also have the case of Naaman, the captain of the Aramean army. We read in 2 Kings Chapter Five that he was a leper who came to the prophet Elisha seeking to be cured of his leprosy. When Naaman arrived at the prophet's home, he was told to go and wash himself seven times in the river Jordan. He immediately became furious (revealing his rebellion) and refused to go. We read:

"So he turned and went away in a rage . . .

"Then his servants came near and spoke to him and said, 'My father, had the prophet told you to do some great thing, would you not have done it? How much more then, when he says to you, "Wash and be clean?"' So he went down and dipped himself seven times in the Jordan, according to the word of the man of God; and his flesh was restored like the flesh of a little child, and he was clean." 2 Kings 5:12a, 13-14

In obedience to God's command (through Elisha), Naaman was cleansed. However, the story doesn't end here. Naaman wanted to reward Elisha for his involvement in his cleansing, but the prophet refused.

Meanwhile, Elisha's servant Gehazi had a rebellious heart. Gehazi secretly ran after Naaman asking for some silver and clothes. Lying to Naaman, Gehazi said that Elisha had sent him and that the money and clothes were for two sons of the prophets. After being given the gifts, Gehazi lied again when Elisha asked him where he had been.

"Gehazi replied, 'Your servant went nowhere.'" (verse 25)

The story ends with Elisha telling Gehazi that the leprosy of Naaman would cleave to him and his descendants forever. When Gehazi left, he had the disease—his skin was as white as snow. Clearly, his rebellion against his master's orders was the root cause of his leprosy.

Another example showing the connection between rebellion and leprosy is found in the life of King Uzziah. We read that King Uzziah was a man who sought the Lord, and in return God prospered him. But as he prospered, Uzziah's heart grew proud.

> "Hence his fame spread afar, for he was marvelously helped until he was strong. But when he became strong, his heart was so proud that he acted corruptly, and he was unfaithful to the Lord his God, for he entered the temple of the Lord to burn incense on the altar of incense." 2 Chronicles 26:15-16

The king had no right to assume the role of priest. But because of his pride, he thought he was above the law. We read that some eighty priests, along with Azariah, warned Uzziah not to proceed. Then we read the following:

> "But Uzziah, with a censer in his hand for burning incense, was enraged; and while he was enraged with the priests, the leprosy broke out on his forehead before the priests in the house of the Lord beside the altar of incense." (verse 19)

Clearly, Uzziah's rebellion (rage) against God's priests brought about his leprosy. Uzziah spent the rest of his life as a leper.

Now one final illustration. This time it is not a rebellious *individual*, but rather a rebellious *nation*, Israel. We read these words in the first chapter of the book of the prophet Isaiah:

"Listen, heavens, and hear, earth;
For the Lord has spoken:

"'Sons I have raised and brought up,
But they have revolted against Me.
An ox knows its owner,
And a donkey its master's manger,
But Israel does not know,
My people do not understand.'
Oh, sinful nation,
People weighed down with guilt,
Offspring of evildoers,
Sons who act corruptly!
They have abandoned the Lord,
They have despised the Holy One of Israel,
They have turned away from Him.
Where will you be stricken again,
As you continue in your rebellion?
The entire head is sick
And the entire heart is faint.
From the sole of the foot even to the head
There is nothing healthy in it,
Only bruises, slashes, and raw wounds;
Not pressed out nor bandaged,
Nor softened with oil."
Isaiah 1:2-6

The prophet here described Israel as a leper, covered in sores from head to toe. He begged them not to continue in their rebellion but to wash themselves.

"Wash yourselves, make yourselves clean;
Remove the evil of your deeds from My sight.
Stop doing evil, learn to do good . . ."

Now here is where there has come some great misunderstanding. The prophet continues with these familiar words:

> "'Come now, and let us reason together,' says
> the Lord, 'Though your sins are as scarlet,
> They shall become as white as snow;
> Though they are red like crimson,
> They shall be like wool.
> If you are willing and obedient,
> You will eat the best of the land;
> But if you refuse and rebel,
> You will be devoured by the sword.'
> For the mouth of the Lord has spoken."
> (verses 18-20)

The common interpretation is that if they repent of their rebellion, they will become as white as snow. But what the prophet is really saying is, "Let's talk about what you are doing. If you keep going in the direction you are heading, things are only going to get worse." He's likening the nation to a leper in the early stages. Leprosy begins with a red rising in the skin. (That sounds like someone getting angry, doesn't it?) But when leprosy is full blown, it turns as white as snow. Remember Miriam, Gehazi, and King Uzziah? They became as white as snow. Now let's read this again:

> "'Come now, and let us reason together,' says
> the Lord, 'Though your sins are as scarlet,
> They shall become as white as snow . . .'"

It seems to me that God is trying to stop His people from continuing in their rebellion, so that He doesn't have to isolate them entirely, as He would with a leper whose leprosy has turned white.

Here are some interesting facts about leprosy and rebellion:

Leprosy is spread by the mucus from the nose or mouth. Rebellion is spread by word of mouth.

Leprosy caused the members of the body to become insensitive to all feeling and caused them to wither away. Rebellion can also cause those members in the Body of Christ to become insensitive to other members, and cause them to leave the church body.

Leprosy was the only sickness or disease where the person was told to go back to the priest to be pronounced clean. Those involved in rebellion against authority also need to go to the ones in authority to be forgiven.

Finally, if a person has a case of leprosy they had to be put out of the camp. Those involved in rebellion must also be disciplined for the sake of the overall health of the Church. I have taken perhaps a little too much time to deal with this matter of rebellion, but we need to understand its seriousness.

After having made sure that we have not allowed any rebellion to creep into our lives, then we can clothe ourselves with the full armor of God.

THE SWORD OF THE SPIRIT

While we are never told to take off the armor, I do believe we need to remind ourselves of what the Lord has provided for us. Remember, it's the armor of God; His salvation, His righteousness, His truth, His sword and shield, etc. As the writer of Proverbs reminds us:

> . . ."the righteous are as bold as a lion."
> Proverbs 28:1

While the majority of the armor is *defensive* in nature, there's one *offensive* weapon: the Sword of the Spirit, which is the Word of God. This fact was brought to my attention in a very vivid way some years ago. My wife and I, along with our youngest daughter at the time, were invited to travel from our home in New Zealand to Penang, Malaysia. I was asked to teach in some morning sessions, as well as minister in the evening services. We stayed in the home of a wonderful Chinese doctor and his family. One afternoon the Doctor asked if I would like to watch a video of a lady by the name of Suzette Hatting. I found out that

Suzette was the prayer coordinator for all of Reinhard Bonnke's worldwide crusades.

The video was recorded at Kensington Temple, a large church in London. Suzette's topic was *spiritual warfare*. While speaking, she called upon one of the young leaders and then clothed him in a coat of armor that she had brought along. The armor was only made of plastic, but it provided a great visual for all who were watching.

After explaining the importance of each piece of armor, Suzette handed the young man a sword and announced that they were about to fight. Suzette said she would play the role of *the devil* and he would play the role of *the believer*.

Suzette had a dagger, and she began to stab repeatedly at her opponent. The young man instinctively raised his shield and kept doing so throughout the whole episode (which lasted less than a minute) before Suzette stopped him. She then turned to the congregation and said, "See? He's like most believers; he never used his sword once!"

I've repeated this story many times over the years, and I've told congregations all over the world that it was worth my entire trip to Malaysia just to be reminded of our need to use our sword! The Sword of the Spirit is a powerful weapon but only if we use it. An unused sword is completely useless.

Jesus repeatedly used the Sword of the Spirit when He was confronted by the devil in the wilderness. In saying this, I don't want in any way to convey that the shield is not important. Both sword and shield have their respective roles.

Before moving on, let me ask you a question: What is the difference between taking up the Sword of the Spirit, which is the Word of God, and our *loins being girded about with truth*? Don't *truth* and *the word* imply the same thing? We know from Scripture that the sum total of God's Word is referred to as *truth*. Jesus said, "I am the way, *the truth* . . ."

A soldier carried his sword in a scabbard, or sheath, which was attached to his body by a belt. When needed, he would draw his sword. In like manner, we need to know God's truth, so that when confronted with temptation we can draw our sword from that belt of truth and use it as a weapon against the enemy. It's not enough to just randomly quote Scripture. We need to have a *rhema* word (specific word) drawn from the logos (totality) of truth. When Jesus was confronted by the devil in the wilderness (who told him to turn stones into bread), He didn't just quote any verse but one specific to the temptation: . . ."man shall not live by bread alone . . ."

Memorize the Word of God! It will serve you well throughout your entire life.

THE CROSS & BLOOD OF CHRIST

Of all the weapons the Lord has given us, the foundational weapon is *the blood* or *the Cross*. Every other weapon depends upon the victory of the Cross. Without the shedding of blood, not only is there no forgiveness of sin, there is no possible victory over the powers of darkness. John reminds us that Jesus came not only to save us from sin but also to destroy the works of the devil:

"The Son of God appeared for this purpose to destroy the works of the devil." 1 John 3:8

Paul also reminds us:

"And when you were dead in your transgressions and the uncircumcision of your flesh, He made us alive together with Him having forgiven us all our transgressions, having cancelled out the certificate of debt consisting of decrees against us and which were hostile to us; and He has taken it out of the way, having nailed it to the cross. When He had disarmed the rulers and authorities, He made a public display of them, having triumphed over them through Him." Colossians 2:13-15

The triumph of the Cross is the foundation for every other weapon!

The apostle John wrote in Revelation that they overcame the accuser (Satan) *"because of the blood of the Lamb."* (Revelation 12:11)

It is important that we understand this verse correctly. Too many people think the blood is a sort of protective charm. You hear them say, "I plead the blood," or "I cover you [or myself] with the blood." While I'm sure the Lord understands our childish error, we need to read the verse correctly: . . . "because of the blood." In other words, we are to remind the adversary of the cross and what Christ accomplished through His death.

Allow me to illustrate it this way: slavery ended in America with the *Emancipation Proclamation,* which was signed into law by President Lincoln in 1863. Any slaves in the Confederacy at that time were granted their freedom based on the law. They didn't literally have to take the parchment the law was written upon and thrust it in the face of their master. They simply declared that because of what President Lincoln signed into law they were free.

Likewise, two thousand years ago Jesus Christ, God's Son, paid the penalty for our sins and also destroyed the works of the devil. Therefore, because of Christ's finished work, we can remind the devil of his defeat.

You recall how God provided deliverance to His people Israel when they were in Egypt. He told Moses to tell the people to take a lamb, slay it, and apply the blood on the doorpost and lintel of their houses. The blood provided protection from death but also served as a *type* of salvation. Not only were they redeemed by the blood of the lamb, but they were spared from the judgement of death.

This Feast of Passover was fulfilled by Christ on the cross. What is interesting to note, however, is that when we read of the first Passover account, God declared to Moses:

> "I will go through the land of Egypt on that night, and will strike down all the first-born in the land of Egypt, both man and beast; and against all the gods of Egypt I will execute judgements—I am the Lord." Exodus 12:12

God made it clear to Moses that He was going to bring judgment upon all the *gods* of Egypt that night, declaring Himself as Lord.

When we partake of the Lord's Supper, or Communion, we should recognize that the emblems of the cup and the bread speak not only of our forgiveness of sin but also of the Lord's victory over every demonic realm. "Do this in remembrance of Me" not only reminds us of our deliverance but also of our enemy's defeat. Years ago, an intercessor friend of mine told me that the Lord revealed to him that the Lord's Table or Communion is one of the greatest weapons to use against the enemy. The devil hates any mention of the blood.

THE WORD OF OUR TESTIMONY

The word of our testimony is also a powerful weapon against the enemy. We can declare that we are blood bought and are no longer a part of the devil's kingdom. We declare that we are a son or daughter of the Living God and that the Spirit of God dwells within us. When we make these declarations, we need to do so with conviction and faith, as whatever is not of faith is sin.

THE NAME OF JESUS

Another weapon that the enemy fears is the Name of Jesus. His name carries authority. Jesus stated:

... "in My name they will cast out devils . . ."
Mark 16:17

We read in Paul's letter to the Philippians:

"Therefore, also God highly exalted Him, and bestowed on Him the name which is above every name, that at the name of Jesus EVERY KNEE SHOULD BOW, of things in heaven, and on earth, and under the earth, and that every tongue should confess that Jesus Christ is Lord, to the glory of God the Father." Philippians 2:9-11 (emphasis mine)

As God's beloved children, we have the right to use His name. When the prodigal son returned to his father's house, he was given the best robe, signifying cleansing and sonship. But he was also given a ring. The ring was not merely a piece of jewelry but the equivalent today of a credit card. The ring bore the master's seal, or crest, and could be used with the full backing and authority of his father.

In those days a merchant would list whatever was being purchased or ordered on a tablet with a coating of wax. The one making the purchase would press his ring into the wax, leaving the equivalent of his signature on the tablet. We too have been given the honor of using the name of Jesus, and the full authority of heaven stands behind that name.

✝ NINE ✝

Standing on God's Promises

After making weapons in great numbers, Hezekiah gathered his military officers in the city square and encouraged them.

We all tend to become discouraged when under attack. What's so interesting about Hezekiah's encouragement is that he didn't just speak his own glib words. He encouraged his men with actual promises from God's Word—which has God's backing and carries far more weight than our own words.

One of the essential reasons we have God's Word is that "through perseverance and the encouragement of the Scriptures we might have hope." (Romans 15:4)

When Hezekiah addressed his military leaders, here is what he said:

"Be strong and courageous, do not fear or be dismayed because of the king of Assyria, nor because of all the multitude which is with him; for the one with us is greater than the one with him. With him is only an arm of flesh, but with us is the Lord our God to help us and to fight our battles." 2 Chronicles 32:7-8

Now let's look at where Hezekiah found that promise. We read in Deuteronomy 20:1-4 these words:

"When you go out to battle against your enemies and see horses and chariots more numerous than you, do not be afraid of them; for the Lord your God who brought you out of Egypt is with you. Now it shall come about when you are approaching the battle, the priest shall come near and speak to the people. And he shall say to them, "hear O Israel, you are approaching the battle against your enemies today. Do not be fainthearted. Do not be afraid, or panic, or tremble before them. For the Lord your God is the one who goes with you, to fight for you against your enemies, to save you."

Hezekiah was well-versed in God's promises. He knew how to draw the Sword of the Spirit and use it effectively against any potential form of discouragement or fear.

ENCOURAGED BY GOD'S WORD

God's Word is not just a collection of stories and events compiled from numerous authors but having little or no relevance to our everyday lives. Rather it contains *everything that pertains to life and godliness*.

In his second epistle, Peter wrote:

> "Grace and peace be multiplied to you in the knowledge of God and of Jesus Christ our Lord; seeing that His divine power has granted us everything pertaining to life and godliness through the true knowledge of Him who called us by His own glory and excellence." 2 Peter 1:2-3

God reveals Himself to us through His Word. While I do believe God can reveal Himself through dreams, visions, trances, etc. His primary way is through His Word. Anything that stands in contradiction to His Word is unreliable and should be immediately rejected as false.

The more we saturate ourselves in the Word of God, the more effective we will be in our ability to overcome the enemy. God's Word is our spiritual food, by which we grow into *Christlikeness*.

Without a balanced diet we become weak and anemic, which can lead to sickness and eventually death.

The same thing is true spiritually. A weak Christian is more susceptible to deception, discouragement and, yes, even death.

Jesus shared with His disciples a parable about a sower sowing his seed. The obvious intent of the sower was to increase the seed sown. The seed, according to Matthew's gospel, was the "word of the kingdom." The sower refers to the Lord Himself, or King Jesus, who is seeking to establish His kingdom in our hearts. The devil seeks to do whatever he can to thwart that purpose.

In the case of some, the devil comes immediately to snatch away the seed before it can take root. In the lives of others, he applies pressure in the form of affliction, persecution, or even ridicule; his desire is that they wither and fall away.

For those who are able to resist and endure the attack of the birds of prey and times of persecution, he changes his tactics again, tempting them to focus on the riches and worries of life. If they fall for his trick, they never bring fruit to maturity. While they may not fall away like the others, neither do they attain to God's purpose of bearing fruit. After all, the intent of the sower was to increase His kingdom. And indeed, some seed increased thirtyfold, some sixtyfold, and others a hundredfold.

This parable reveals a conflict between the Kingdom of God and the kingdom of Satan. It also reveals the various ways in which the enemy operates. God's Word is your spiritual food, by which you grow and produce a harvest—and the devil's goal is to prevent that from happening. He comes in three ways:

As a roaring lion,
As a wolf in sheep's clothing,
And finally, as an angel of light.

I suggest you study this parable on your own with this in mind. Remember that God will reveal Himself to you through His Word but only *if you read it*. The more you saturate yourself with the Word of God, the more you will be able to withstand the attacks of the enemy—and this is precisely why the devil will try to keep you away from God's Word!

ENCOURAGED BY BIBLE CHARACTERS

One of my favorite topics is the study of Bible characters. Each person recorded in the Word of God is real, warts and all. In other words, God doesn't airbrush these people by removing all their imperfections. If He did, imagine how discouraging reading the Bible would be. My good friend Winkie Pratney would often shock his audience by telling them that the Bible is full of mistakes. Then, having their full attention, he would quickly add, "It records Adam's mistake, Noah's mistake, David's mistake, etc. In other words, the Bible is full of *before and after* stories, all recorded by the Holy Spirit for our encouragement and hope."

Take Peter for example: Peter boasted that he would never deny his master; he would die before doing so! I'm convinced that Peter really believed he had enough willpower to remain faithful no matter what. You can imagine how he felt when Jesus warned him that he would deny him three times before the cock crowed.

Sure enough, the night that Judas betrayed Jesus, Peter denied three times that he even knew his Lord. While warming himself around an open fire, he repeatedly denied knowing the Lord. Then the cock crowed, and Peter's self-confidence plummeted. I can only imagine how he must have felt during the next few days, knowing he had failed his Lord so miserably.

Overwhelmed by discouragement, Peter returned to fishing and convinced some of the other disciples to join him. After a fruitless night of fishing, he no doubt felt worse, thinking, *I can't even catch fish anymore!* Suddenly, Jesus appeared and instructed them to cast their net one more time. Almost instantaneously, the net was filled with fish and was too heavy to be lifted. John then realized it was the Lord. Peter immediately stripped himself and dove into the sea trying to reach Jesus.

On shore, Jesus had already prepared a fire; he told the disciples to bring him some of their catch so they could have breakfast together. In John's record of this event, we're told that this was the third time Jesus had appeared to His disciples following His resurrection.

What happened next is deeply moving. Here were the disciples, standing around a charcoal fire, and Jesus said to Peter, "Simon, son of John, do you love me more than these?"

Peter replied, "Yes, Lord."

Three times Jesus asked Peter the same question. And three times Peter professed that he did love Jesus. Why three times? Jesus was not only forgiving Peter for denying Him three times, but He was also allowing Peter to *make amends* for his denials. For each time that Peter had denied the Lord, the Lord allowed Peter to reaffirm his love for Him.

We see a similar case in the Old Testament story of the prophet Jonah. Jonah was told explicitly by God to go to Nineveh, but he rebelled and decided to go to Tarshish instead. Jonah's disobedience cost him dearly, as we know. Following his three days and three nights in the belly of some great sea monster, and after repenting, we read this of Jonah:

> "Now the word of the Lord came to Jonah the second time saying, 'Arise, go to Nineveh . . .'"
> Jonah 3:1-2

This verse has brought fresh hope and encouragement to numerous believers who have failed or disobeyed God in some way. Yes, God is the God of the second chance! I'm often reminded of my years in school, where the teacher would give us the opportunity to take a test over again if we had failed. God also allows us to do *make-up tests.*

Keep in mind that these biblical accounts were written for our instruction, to give us hope. God's Word is filled with promises and examples of forgiveness, restoration, and hope—but also with warnings about the consequences of sin and disobedience.

In closing this chapter, allow me to refresh your memory with what Moses told the children of Israel just prior to his death:

> "Take to your heart all the words with which I am warning you today, which you shall com-

mand your sons to observe carefully, even all the words of this law. For it is not an idle word for you, indeed it is your life. And by this word you shall prolong your days in the land . . ." Deuteronomy 32:46-47

Learn to treasure God's Word; it is indeed your life. It holds the answer to every question, need, and dilemma that will come your way. God's Word never becomes obsolete or outdated. It will never fail you or disappoint you.

. . ."you have exalted your word above all your name." Psalm 138:2

† TEN †

Overcoming Discouragement

Let's return to Hezekiah and his battle against the Assyrian army. We have already learned a great deal from the way Hezekiah prepared to confront the enemy.

The water supply was cut off, the walls were repaired, and the towers erected. Weapons were made and readied, and, finally, the king encouraged his leaders with the promises of God.

The next thing we read is that Sennacherib sent his servants to Jerusalem to mock, belittle, and ridicule the children of God for putting their trust in God. Sennacherib's servants reminded God's people that at one time they had *many gods* to call on; but Hezekiah had done away with them and left them with only one God. In the eyes of the enemy, this was a foolish decision. Little did they know that the "one remaining God" was *the Living God*, the Lord of lords, and King of kings!

Sennacherib's servants continued to mock and make fun of Hezekiah's decision to rely upon God for help; they boasted of all the nations they had already conquered. Listen to their words of intimidation:

> "'Do you not know what I and my fathers have done to all the peoples of the lands? Were the gods of the nations of the lands able at all to deliver their land from my hand? Who was there among all the gods of those nations which my fathers utterly destroyed who could deliver his people out of my hands, that your God should be able to deliver you from my hand? Who was there among all the gods of those nations which my fathers utterly destroyed who could deliver his people out of my hands, that your God should be able to deliver you from my hand? ...
>
> "How much less shall your God deliver you from my hand?' He also wrote letters to insult the Lord God of Israel, and to speak against Him, saying 'As the gods of the nations of the lands have not delivered their people from my hand, so the God of Hezekiah shall not deliver His people from my hand.'"
>
> 2 Chronicles 32:13-15,17

These same tactics are still used against us today by the devil and his demonic hordes. He seeks to intimidate us by magnifying and exalting himself; he reminds us of all those he has already destroyed, deceived, or discouraged. Not only that, but he will shout in your ear that God is powerless to help you.

In response to these discouraging threats, we read in the book of Isaiah of another helpful step that Hezekiah employed against this unrelenting torrent of verbal fear mongering:

> "But they were silent and answered him not a word, for the king's command was, 'Do not answer him.'" Isaiah 36:21

In other words, don't listen to the lies of the enemy! Remember, Satan is a liar and the father of lies. He will remind you of your past and seek to use that against you. When this happens, begin thanking the Lord for His forgiveness and cleansing.

Your past is forgiven and you are no longer his captive, but you are a liberated son or daughter of the Living God. Everything the enemy tells you is a lie meant to deceive, discourage, and destroy you.

Read God's Word and immerse yourself in the truth. It will set you free.

CONDEMNATION VS. CONVICTION

One final note, which I trust will be of help to you. Learn to discern the difference between *condemnation* and *conviction*. Years ago I was listening to a recording of Pastor Jack Hayford, who explained how to tell if you were under *condemnation* or *conviction*. I believe he credited his brother with the insight that he shared.

Condemnation he said, is when the devil dredges up some sin or past failure in your life, and he proceeds to dangle it in front of you to keep you from making spiritual progress. The enemy attempts to use our past against us for the purpose of destroying any hope for the future. Condemnation is that feeling of having a heavy cloud come over you that provides you with no exit. It just tends to linger over you and drain you of your peace and joy.

Conviction, on the other hand, is when the Holy Spirit reaches into some *unconfessed* area of your life and reveals it to you—so that you can experience God's forgiveness, and thereby face the future with hope. Conviction, unlike condemnation, provides you with an *exit*, some specific sin the Lord wants to forgive you of, free you from, and remove from your life.

† ELEVEN †
Pray, Pray, Pray!

We now turn to the last recorded act of Hezekiah—prayer! You may ask the question, (and rightly so) why did Hezekiah wait so long before asking God for His help? While he may have prayed prior to this, he has now completed some necessary *prerequisites* for prayer.

Repentance is one of those prerequisites. There are certain things that God expects us to do, and He will work alongside us. It is our responsibility to repent, or cut off those areas of our life that provide grounds for the enemy. God expects us to resist the enemy, and He expects us to read His Word, etc.

Not only did Hezekiah pray, but he prayed with the prophet Isaiah. This shows a great deal of humility on the part of Hezekiah. After all, he was the king; he could have allowed pride to keep him from seeking help. Don't ever allow pride to rob you of another's help! God's Word tells us that two are better than one:

"One will chase a thousand and two put ten thousand to flight." Deuteronomy 32:30

I recently read the following about the pulling strength of two horses' verses one:

"A single draft horse can pull a load up to 8,000 pounds. The strength involved in this is hard to imagine ...

"Two trained horses in tandem can actually pull 32,000 pounds, which is a load four times as heavy as either of the horses could pull by themselves." (*"Horse Sense," Jim Stovall*)

While we don't need science to prove our point, it does show how much more effective two are than one. We read that Hezekiah not only prayed, but he "cried out to heaven." (verse 20)

Given the circumstances, I can well believe that Hezekiah wasn't just whispering quiet platitudes but rather raising his voice in desperation. His very city, people, and life were being threatened.

My father, who was a man of prayer, would often say, "God doesn't answer prayer, He only answers desperate prayer."

The account we read in Second Chronicles tells us that he prayed, but it doesn't reveal anything else about his prayer. Isaiah's account, while not as detailed about the king's circumstances, gives us his actual prayer. Here it is:

> "And Hezekiah prayed to the Lord saying, 'O Lord of Hosts, the God of Israel, who art enthroned above the cherubim, Thou art the Lord, Thou alone of all the kingdoms of the earth. Thou hast made heaven and earth. Incline Thine ear, O Lord, and hear; open Thine eyes, O Lord, and see; and listen to all the words of Sennacherib who sent them to reproach the living God. Truly, O Lord, the kings of Assyria have devastated all the countries and their lands, and have cast their gods into the fire, for they were not gods but the work of men's hands, wood and stone. So they have destroyed them. And now, O Lord our God, deliver us from his hand that all the kingdoms of the earth may know that Thou alone Lord, art God.'" Isaiah 37:15-20

What an amazing prayer! It provides us with so much insight on how to pray. The first thing we learn is that he addressed his prayer *to the Lord*. The Hebrew word used here is *Jehovah*. Since I make no claim to know or understand Hebrew or Greek, I have to rely on other sources. I carry in my personal Bible a copy of a page from G. Campbell Morgan's book *The Ten Commandments*. In this book, he gives some great insight into God's name, Jehovah; and I quote:

"THE NAME OF GOD:

There's deep significance in the name by which God here declares Himself, JEHOVAH. It is a combination of three Hebrew words, which may be translated into an English form thus: Yehi, "He will be," Hove, "being," and Hahyah, "He was." A combination is made from the three words by taking the first syllable of the first YE-Hi, the middle syllable of the second, hOVe, and the last syllable of the third, hahyAH, so that we have the name YEHOVAH. The whole name means, "He that will be. He that is, He that was." Thus the very name brings man into the presence of the Supreme, the Eternal, the Self-existent God, Who is because He is—a great and perpetual mystery to the finite mind of man, and for the most part beyond all human analysis. If the mind reach out to the limitless stretches of future generations, God says, "I am He that will be." If men think of the present moment, with all its marvelous manifestations of life and order and mystery and revelation, God says, "I am He that is." If the mind be carried as far back as possible into infinite spaces of the past, God says, "I am He that was." Whether man thinks of his origin, of his present condition, or of his future destiny, God says, "I AM."

Hezekiah addresses his prayer to the eternal, everlasting, and yet present God. We too can bring our needs before the God of Abraham, Isaac, and Jacob—the same God that Adam had communion with in the garden; the same God that Enoch walked with for over three hundred years; the God of Elijah and Elisha, etc. What a great honor and privilege to come into the presence of the I AM!

Hezekiah then begins his prayer:

"O Lord of hosts, the God of Israel . . ."

This could be translated "Lord of armies," referring to the angelic realm or simply to the heavens. Either way, we can grasp the magnitude of God's creation and power.

What is so interesting about this particular phrase is that God very literally dispatched an angel in response to his prayer. Speaking of what happened to Hezekiah's enemy Sennacherib, we read:

"And the Lord sent an angel who destroyed every mighty warrior, commander, and officer in the camp of the king of Assyria. So he returned in shame to his own land. And when he entered the temple of his god, some of his own children killed him there with the sword."
2 Chronicles 32:21

Hezekiah understood the supernatural realm and God's authority over the armies of heaven. God remains the Lord of hosts and has assigned His angels as ministering spirits to each and every believer.

HEAVEN'S LANGUAGE

Allow me, if you will, to insert here some thoughts on the gift of tongues. I'm well aware of the fact that this topic has caused as much division and controversy as any other single topic in Scripture. The Apostle Paul made clear in his letter to the Corinthians: "do not forbid to speak in tongues." (1 Cor. 14:39) Paul gave his own testimony, telling us: "I speak in tongues more than you all." (1 Cor. 14:18) And finally he states: "Now I wish that you all spoke in tongues." (1 Cor. 14:5)

What is it about this gift that raises so much controversy? God obviously knew what He was doing when He gave it. After all:

> "Every good thing given and every perfect gift is from above, coming down from the Father of lights, with whom there is no variation or shifting shadow." James 1:17

The Scriptures make it clear that when a believer speaks in tongues, he edifies himself:

"One who speaks in tongues edifies himself." 1 Cor. 14:4

Speaking in tongues is like a spiritual tonic for the soul. But let me get to the point I wish to make: some years ago I asked myself the question, *Why would the Spirit of God allow me to speak in the tongues of angels?* I can understand being given an earthly tongue, as presumably it would allow me to speak to someone who is a native to that language. But why the *tongue of an angel?*

Tongues—or languages—are the means by which we communicate. The Chinese speak Mandarin or Cantonese; the French speak French; the Spaniards speak Spanish, etc. So if I speak in the tongue of an angel, I must be communicating in an *angelic language*—one that angels understand. That being true, I also know that we are *not* to worship angels. The Apostle John tells us:

> "I fell down to worship at the feet of an angel, who showed me these things. And he said to me, 'Do not do that, I am a fellow servant of yours and of your brethren the prophets and of those who heed the words of this book; worship God.'" Revelation 22:8-9

The book of Hebrews confirms the fact that angels are heavenly servants:

"Are they not all ministering spirits, sent out to render service for the sake of those who will inherit salvation." Hebrews 1:14

Scripture establishes the role of angels as servants, on our behalf. Therefore, wouldn't it stand to reason that the Holy Spirit, speaking through us, is serving notice to the angelic realm to come to our aid in some way?

Tongues is the language of heaven. I'm convinced that when we pray in tongues, the Spirit of God is issuing orders to the angelic realm to go to battle on our behalf.

Finally, allow me this disclaimer: I don't want to be dogmatic about this, and thereby cause even more division—but neither do I want to avoid it, and thereby deprive us of what could be a vital weapon in our spiritual arsenal. If what I am suggesting is true, then is it any wonder that the devil has tried to level as much criticism and ridicule on this gift than he has on all others combined?

BATTLING THROUGH PRAYER

It reminds me of how the Philistines sought to weaken the Israelites ability to fight by destroying all the blacksmith shops throughout the land of Israel. This is one of the most intriguing stories concerning warfare in the entire Bible. Let me set the scene for you:

One of Israel's fiercest (most frequent) enemies were the Philistines. It was young David who slew Goliath, a Philistine, while Saul and all his men fled from him. Israel and the Philistines were constantly at war. We read in 1 Samuel 13:19-23 this account:

> "Now no blacksmith could be found in all the land of Israel . . .
>
> "So all Israel went down to the Philistines, each to sharpen his plowshare, his mattock, his axe, and his hoe. And the charge was two-thirds of a shekel for the plowshares, the mattocks, the forks, and the axes, and to fix the hoes."

You may wonder what this had to do with *warfare*. The fact is, it had nothing to do with it. Before we delve into this a little deeper, let me explain why this very sinister, cunning, and intriguing plan worked so well.

We are not told why Israel allowed all their blacksmith shops to be sold, destroyed, or removed, but they were oblivious to what was really taking place.

While the Philistines obviously profited from charging Israel to repair or sharpen their agricultural implements, their real motive was far more crafty.

Let me take you back to the story and one specific piece of information I left out:

> "Now no blacksmith could be found in all the land of Israel, for the Philistines said, 'Lest the Hebrews make swords or spears.'"

Here we gain insight into their motivation. The blacksmith shops were scattered throughout Israel and were the source for the manufacturing of their agricultural tools. But they were also the source for the manufacture of their weapons! If you eliminate the places where the weapons are made, you also eliminate their ability to use them. So effective was their plan that we read the following:

> "So it came about on the day of battle that neither sword nor spear was found in the hands of any of the people who were with Saul and Jonathan, but they were found with Saul and his son Jonathan."

It is my personal conviction that long ago Satan concocted a plan to eliminate the prayer meeting from the house of God, thereby destroying the use of our spiritual weapons, and virtually rendering the Church powerless.

Not only has the enemy been successful corporately but also individually. It's time we restored the blacksmith shop in our own lives, as well as the church.

DELIGHTING IN PRAYER

Hezekiah continued with his prayer, stating: . . . "the God of Israel, who art enthroned above the cherubim." The mention of the cherubim serves to remind Hezekiah that God was present in the temple there in the city of Jerusalem as well as in the heavens above. In other words, He's *our God* or *my God*. We too need to grasp both of these truths.

Jesus reminds us that *our Father which art in heaven* is also the one who will never leave us or forsake us. When we read, "Our Father which art in heaven," Jesus wasn't referring to the Father being in some distant galaxy; rather He was referring to God being *on the throne*.

We read in Isaiah 66:1 and Acts 7:49:

> "Heaven is My throne and the earth is My footstool."

Jesus reminded us of this again when He stated, "Make no oath at all, either by heaven, for it is the throne of God."

God's throne speaks to us of His power, authority, and sovereignty. God is not some impotent god but the omnipotent ruler of heaven and earth.

Hezekiah then acknowledged that God is the only God and ruler "of all the kingdoms of the earth." If we truly grasp these truths, then prayer ceases to be a burden and becomes a delight.

He continues by saying, "Thou hast made heaven and earth." History records many rulers of kingdoms, but none of them could make the claim of being *creator* of those kingdoms! Our God alone is the Creator of all things.

PRAYING FOR HELP

Having acknowledged God's awesomeness, Hezekiah then asked for help. God is never troubled or bothered by our cry for help. He tells us to call upon Him; He is a present help in time of trouble.

If only we would take Him up on His offer to help us; what a difference that would make in our trials and temptations. He tells us to cast our burdens and cares upon Him, for He cares for us. Do you believe that?

PRAYING TO GLORIFY GOD

Hezekiah closes his prayer by telling the Lord that he is motivated by one thing:

. . . "that all the kingdoms of the earth may know that Thou alone Lord art God."

Hezekiah was not seeking his own glory or honor but was motivated by one desire: that God alone be magnified and made known to every kingdom on earth. This should be what motivates us as we pray.

As we learn to lay hold of God through prayer, we will discover that He will empower us to overcome those areas of difficulty or bondage that once held us captive. Then, having been set free by overcoming, we can begin to focus on finding and fulfilling the will of God for our lives.

A LIFE OF PRAYER

Prayer should become a daily part of our walk with the Lord. While He responds to our cries for help, He also longs to fellowship with us and to become our friend—and we, His friends.

We read in Mark's gospel what prompted the disciples of Jesus to ask Him to teach them how to pray: They had been watching Jesus pray.

I believe they realized that the secret to their Master's supernatural life was directly tied to His life of prayer. No sooner had He finished praying than they approached Him and said to Him, "Lord, teach us to pray . . ." Luke's account of what is commonly referred to as "The Lord's Prayer" is shorter than that recorded in Matthew Chapter Six.

Since Jesus uttered these words two thousand years ago, Matthew's account has been repeated millions upon millions of times by believers and non-believers. Many biblical expositors believe that this was never intended to be used as a *prayer but* rather as an *outline for prayer*. The rabbis referred to it as an *index prayer,* meaning it gave us an order or outline for how to pray. Perhaps the best way to explain this is to share my personal outline with you. You may want to follow this, or use your own:

THE LORD'S PRAYER

HIS PERSON: Our Father
HIS POSITION: Which art in heaven
HIS PREEMINENCE: Hallowed be Thy name
HIS POWER: Thy Kingdom come
HIS PURPOSE: Thy will be done
HIS PATTERN: On earth as it is in heaven
HIS PROVISION: Give us this day our daily bread
HIS PARDON: And forgive us our debts
HIS PRINCIPLE: As we forgive our debtors
HIS PROTECTION: And do not lead us into temptation, but deliver us from evil
HIS PRAISE: For Thine is the kingdom and the power, and the glory, forever, Amen

When we dissect this prayer in this way, we can better understand why the rabbis referred to it as an *index* prayer. It was meant to provide the one praying with *topics* to pray about, not just words to be repeated.

FORGIVENESS AND PRAYER

The topic of prayer is endless, and it is not my intention to elaborate on it, as there are numerous books available if you would like to study further on it.

What I do want to do, before we move on from "The Lord's Prayer," is to draw your attention to what Jesus said immediately after giving His disciples this pattern of prayer. Jesus could have easily gone back and underscored the importance of His Kingdom, or of His will being done on earth. But instead He chose to underscore the importance of *forgiveness*. This is what He said:

> "For if you forgive men for their transgressions, your heavenly Father will also forgive you. But if you do not forgive men, then your Father will not forgive your transgressions." Matthew 6:14-15

In Chapter Six I mentioned that I would deal with the matter of *unforgiveness* later. My reason for doing so is that I believe holding onto unforgiveness is one of the greatest obstacles to personal freedom and (for that matter) personal revival.

You could call unforgiveness an *unpardonable sin*. Simply speaking, if we fail to forgive, then we cannot be forgiven; in other words, our sin is unpardonable.

Now I'm not trying to be sensational or make a definitive statement regarding the unpardonable sin; I'm simply trying to stress the importance of forgiveness. With that in mind, I've added a separate book on this topic.

BoOk TwO

Book Two

✝ ONE ✝
Unforgiven!

The title of this chapter may sound confusing, especially if you've been raised with the belief that once you're forgiven, your sins cannot be reinstated.

Some would say that to suggest that our loving heavenly Father would revoke our forgiveness is tantamount to heresy. Why would God reinstate our sins? Doesn't God's Word promise us that if we confess our sins, He is faithful and just to forgive us our sins? The idea that God would break His promise undermines the very foundation of our Christian faith.

Or does it?

Before you jump to the conclusion that this is some type of false doctrine, take time to find out the truth. After all, if what you have just read is true, then you should know *why* God would do such a thing. Since your eternal life depends on whether you have been forgiven or not, it's vital that you know for sure.

There's an old saying that says: *Your enemy will tell you what your friends won't.* For example, your enemy may just blurt out that you have terrible breath, while your friends remain silent, hoping somebody else will tell you. However, even though that old saying has a bit of truth in it, we know that a true friend will tell you the truth regardless. And hearing the truth may embarrass us initially, but deep down we appreciate being told the truth.

Jesus is the greatest friend imaginable—He's a friend who sticks closer than any sibling; a friend who gave up His life to save you. Jesus is a friend who will tell you the truth even though it may wound you temporarily.

In the following chapters we're going to look into God's Word regarding the topic of forgiveness. There's no greater topic than forgiveness; without it we face the certain and sure fate of eternal agony and separation from God.

✝ TWO ✝
Our Forgiving God

One of the greatest revelations we have of God is the that He forgives. Yes, we can talk about His glorious holiness, His awesome power, and His magnificent majesty. These, along with His unlimited knowledge and wisdom, set Him apart from all other gods. However, these attributes alone would be of little value to us if He didn't forgive!

The Bible makes it clear that our sins have separated us from God. Therefore, without His forgiveness we could never experience Him as our Father and Jesus Christ as our Savior. Throughout the entire Bible, from Genesis to the book of Revelation, we read of God's wonderful grace, mercy, loving-kindness, and forgiveness. I'm well aware of the fact that many believers have been led to believe that the God of the Old Testament is radically different from the God of the New Testament. But nothing could be further from the truth.

When I'm teaching, I sometimes jokingly suggest that the four hundred years of silence (between the Old Testament and the New) was a time where God was attending an intensive class in *anger management*. However, the concept of God being *always on the verge of erupting in anger* is entirely without merit. There's nothing to support this opinion. We know for certain that God is slow to anger—and His anger is forever linked with His justice, mercy, and grace.

One of the great attributes of God is His *unchangeableness*. The Bible states clearly, "I am the Lord and I change not." Forgiveness, then, was not something God added to His portfolio in the New Covenant. Instead, forgiveness has always been the very essence of who He is. Forgiveness is not just something God does but something He delights in doing!

Of forgiveness, the Scriptures make it clear that there's both a *vertical* as well as a *horizontal* aspect, and these two are inseparable. The first concerns our relationship with God, while the second deals with our relationship to others. Only after we've experienced God's forgiveness can we fully release (or forgive) those who have sinned against us. In the following chapter we'll explore God's amazing forgiveness in more detail. Later, and just as importantly, we'll look at our forgiveness of others.

✝ THREE ✝

The Cross: the Basis of Our Forgiveness

There's no greater feeling than being clean. After spending hours working in the garden or tinkering with your car—or simply tiding up around the house—you have that innate desire to be clean. You quickly head for the shower and lather yourself from head to toe with soap. The dirtier you are, the better you feel as the water dissolves all the grease, grime, and dirt. You emerge not only clean but refreshed.

None of us enjoy being dirty. We feel uncomfortable and embarrassed until we decide to shower or bathe. Not only is this true of our bodies but of our cars, houses, clothes, or whatever else is soiled or filthy.

However, there's no comparison with the feeling of being cleansed from sin!

People around the world go to extreme lengths trying to find cleansing from their sinful state. Millions flock to the Ganges River every year, hoping that if they plunge into its filthy water, they can find the peace and cleansing they so desperately long for. Still others make the trek to Mecca or flagellate themselves in the hope of attaining some sense of forgiveness. Some even walk on fire or broken glass in the hope of convincing their god that they are worthy of his forgiveness—only to find that none of these rituals have the power to cleanse their guilty conscience from sin.

The Bible clearly and emphatically declares that *all* have sinned! Not some, or many—not even *most*. All have sinned and fall short.

Sin is universal; it's not exclusive to one nation, tongue, or race. We're all filthy in the eyes of God. Our self-righteousness, or goodness, God considers to be like filthy rags or polluted garments. True forgiveness only has one source: God Himself. This forgiveness is only possible through the atoning work of Jesus Christ. It cannot be earned, bought, bartered, or borrowed. It's not attained by education, experience, or expertise.

Christ's forgiveness is a free gift. However, there are two prerequisites to activate God's forgiveness:

1. Repentance
2. Faith

Without *repentance* there is no acknowledgment of sin, therefore no seeking after forgiveness. Anyone claiming they have no need of repentance is either totally deceived or extremely proud.

And as I've just stated, our forgiveness is only possible through the atoning work of Jesus Christ—in other words, the cross. And to lay hold of the salvation and forgiveness available through the cross requires that we believe in it, or *have faith*.

ATONEMENT

The vast majority of theologians agree that the grandest theme in the entire Bible is that of the atonement. In his exceptional book *The Greatest Theme in the World*, F.E. Marsh opens with this statement:

> "Christ crucified is the greatest theme in the universe, for it proclaims the greatest work ever performed by the greatest Person, and secures the greatest possible ends."

Dr. Hugh McMillan states:

"The Atonement of our Lord is the grandest and most distinctive thing in the Bible—for the sake of which, indeed, the Bible was produced . . . I have no hesitation in saying, the Atonement is not only the greatest fact of Christianity, it is Christianity. It is the supplier of all human need, the answer of all human questions, the minister to all human ills, the joy of all human sorrows, the remover of all human guilt, and the securer of all Divine glory." (citation needed)

The Apostle Paul wrote:

"I delivered to you as of first importance . . . that Christ died for our sins according to the Scriptures." 1 Corinthians 15:3

It's of little wonder then that for the past (almost) two thousand years the *cross* has been the symbol of Christianity. While Roman Catholics focus on the crucifix, we focus on an empty cross—declaring that our God has risen so that we might be forgiven.

In the following chapter we will look at two outstanding incidents of forgiveness, one taken from the Old Testament and one from the New.

† FOUR †

King David Forgiven

When it comes to the matter of forgiveness, people tend to fall into two categories—both of which undermine the work of the cross. The first is the attitude that declares, "I have no need of forgiveness!" The second is a false belief that *because of their past* they can never be forgiven.

Of these two, I'm not sure which is the worst, although I would rather deal with *hopelessness* than *pride*.

When Jesus was confronted by the self-righteous Pharisees he told them:

"It is not those who are well who need a physician but those who are sick . . . I have not come to call the righteous but sinners to repentance." Luke 5:31-32

The sicker you are, the more you're in need of medical attention. No medical professional would ever think of turning you away because you are too sick. Jesus, our Great Physician, has never turned a needy patient away.

TOO SINFUL

Speaking of *feeling your past is too sinful for Jesus to forgive,* Paul (writing to the Romans) told us that the stories of the Old Testament were "written for our instruction, that through perseverance and the encouragement of the Scriptures we might have hope." With that in mind, allow me to take you to the Old Testament and look at just one case that will give you hope.

The story we're going to look at concerns Israel's second king, King David. If you've read the life of this amazing man, you know that he had numerous problems—some of his own making and some from the hands of others. Some Bible scholars believe that David was an illegitimate child. They base this on several scriptures and observations from his life. In

Psalm 51:5 he declared, "In sin did my mother conceive me."

Several times David referred to his mother as a *handmaid* or a servant of some type. It was somewhat common in the Old Testament for a man to marry and have several or more children, and then if his wife was unable to continue having children, he would take one of his wife's *maids* and father children through her.

What lends credence to this idea is seen after Saul's disobedience, when Samuel was told to anoint one of Jesse's sons as king. When Samuel arrived, Jesse (David's father) had already rounded up all of David's brothers—but without letting David know that the prophet Samuel was in town. Can you imagine the feelings of rejection and embarrassment as David saw all of his siblings gathered, and he was never told by his father that the prophet was coming to town?

Samuel, in looking over Jesse's sons, eventually concluded that none of those present was God's choice for king. He then asked Jesse if he had any more sons. Jesse, caught off guard, muttered that he had one more son, the youngest. The word used here to describe David was a belittling term, implying *the least*. In other words, Jesse was thinking David could never amount to much, let alone become king. David had a life of rejection and he learned to cling to God from his birth. He wrote:

> "Upon Thee I was cast from birth; Thou hast been my God from my mother's womb."
> Psalm 22:10

This is just one example of David not having the loving nurture he needed. Samuel anointed David and God promoted him above his brothers, eventually making him king over His people.

We know that David loved God and expressed his love in numerous Psalms. He was a man of prayer who repeatedly sought God's counsel regarding what he was to do, both personally and militarily.

Prior to becoming king, he would lay awake at night wondering how he could return the Ark of God back to its rightful place in the city of Jerusalem. He loved God's presence and referred to it as the "one thing" he desired above all else.

By now you might wonder how a man referred to as "a man after God's heart" could be an example to a sinner like you. However, not only was David a godly man but also a man of *like passions*. He was like you and I. David, like most men, loved women; he married eight wives that we know of. Yes, David loved God, but . . . Well, you get the point.

In 2 Samuel Chapter Eleven, we read the story of one of David's greatest sins. It all began one night when he was unable to sleep and decided to stroll on the balcony of his kingly palace. Some say he should have gone to war with his soldiers—so, he wasn't where he was supposed to be in the first place. However, this was never a hard, fast rule. If a nation's king was killed in battle, that would leave the nation without their leader. Either way, as he was strolling and looking over the rooftops around the palace, he saw a woman bathing. Rather than turning away, he continued to stare and lust after her. Gripped by the thought of lying with her, he summoned her to the palace.

Not long after that incident, the woman (Bathsheba) sent word to David that she was pregnant with his child. We can only imagine what went through David's mind upon hearing the news. Rather than seek God's forgiveness, he immediately tried to cover his sin—he had Bathsheba's husband, Uriah, brought in from the battle. David ordered Uriah to rest and to go visit his wife—hoping the man would lay with her, covering David's sin. But the plan failed. Uriah was a man of integrity and spent the night at the door of the king's palace.

David then decided to throw a party for Uriah in order to get him drunk, hoping that he would then go home to his wife. Again, the plan failed.

At last, David ordered his commander-in-chief, Joab, to place Uriah in the front lines of the battle and then withdraw from him, leaving nothing but certain death as his fate.

When left unchecked, David's sin grew and grew. An initial look gave way to lust; lust gave way to action resulting in adultery, and eventually murder.

HOPE FOR THE REPENTANT

David may have initially consoled himself with the belief that he had gotten away with it, only to find himself flooded with inner torment over his sin. In Psalm 51 we read of David's repentance and forgiveness but not before he acknowledges *"my sin is ever before me."* Whether he was referring to Bathsheba or to his troubled conscience, or both, he could not forget what he had done. Reading a little further on David wrote:

> "Wash me and I will be whiter than snow. Make me to hear joy and gladness, Let the bones which Thou hast broken rejoice."
> Psalm 51:7-8

There's no record of God actually *breaking David's bones;* David's expression probably refers to his deep conviction, likening it to the feeling of having his bones broken.

At last, David reached the point of desperation and finally *came clean.* He held nothing back from God, acknowledging his sin and pleading for forgiveness. He began this Psalm by magnifying God's loving kindness and the greatness of His compassion.

Had David only *acknowledged* his sin, it would have done little or no good. It may have given him a moment of solace but nothing lasting. But David was willing to *repent,* to turn away from his sin and seek forgiveness. If God did not forgive him, he would never find the peace he desperately longed for. The end result was that David, once again, found the "joy of his salvation."

As I stated earlier, Paul told us that these things were written for our instruction, that through the encouragement of the Scriptures, we might *have hope.*

† FIVE †

Sexual Sin Forgiven

We now turn our attention not to an individual but to a group of individuals—the Corinthians! I realize I have already mentioned them, but it bears repeating. My father would often speak of the word *Corinthian* as being the summation of every foul, filthy, despicable, sensuous, perverted, carnal word you could imagine. Today it would be the equivalent of combining every filthy four-letter word imaginable into one single word and then using it to describe someone.

The city of Corinth was known for its immorality and sexual perversion. But thank God, *where sin abounds, grace does much more abound.* It was here in this sin-soaked city that God exhibited His amazing grace and forgiveness.

Paul, when writing to those who had experienced His forgiveness, refers to them as *fornicators, idolaters, adulterers, effeminate, homosexuals, thieves, coveters, drunkards, revilers,* and *swindlers*. Wow! What a list. How would you like to go to a church that was full of former sinners like that? Maybe you would avoid such a group, fearing for your reputation or any potential business associations. Sad but true. However, Paul goes on to say:

> "And such were some of you; but you were washed, but you were sanctified, but you were justified in the name of the Lord Jesus Christ, and in the Spirit of our God." 1 Corinthians 6:11

Hallelujah, what a Savior!

WASHED

Notice Paul uses the word "washed." Can you imagine the joy these men and women must have felt to know that all the filth and sordid sexual uncleanness they had dabbled in was forever gone, and they were pronounced clean? It brings to mind what it must have been like to be a leper in those days, forced to spend your time outside of the city, forever shunned by friends and family, and then to have an encounter with Christ. Suddenly, your decaying flesh is restored to that of a little child; you can't believe your eyes, and you suddenly explode in emotion, unable to contain your joy. You're no longer an outcast! I imagine these Corinthians must have experienced a similar feeling as they passed from "death unto life, and from the power of Satan unto God." But it doesn't end there; there's more to the story.

One evening while living in New Zealand, I was driving and listening to Radio Rhema, New Zealand's only Christian radio station. That evening they were broadcasting a message by Jack Hayford. I don't recall where he gave the message or what the theme of the message was all about. What I do remember, however, was that he referenced a verse from the book of Hebrews that I have never forgotten. In the twenty second verse of Hebrews, Chapter Ten, the writer states that:

"Since we have a great high priest over the house of God, let us draw near with a sincere heart in full assurance of faith, having our hearts sprinkled clean from an evil conscience and our bodies washed with pure water."

Jack Hayford highlighted the latter part of the verse: "our bodies washed." He said there were some listening there who had been involved in sexual activity before marriage that were still feeling the shame and guilt from it. If I recall correctly, he said their sense of still feeling "dirty" was affecting their intimacy in marriage. He concluded by telling his audience that they could have their "bodies washed."

While this may not seem significant to those who have not soiled their bodies, for those who have, it's life transforming. Despite all of man's understanding of psychology, physiology, philosophy, science, medicine, etcetera, they've never discovered a way to "wash" a person whose body was stained by sin. But where man failed, God triumphed!

Remember the Corinthians that Paul spoke of, those who had been involved in every perverted sexual act, including homosexuality? When writing to them a second time, he made this astounding statement:

> "For I am jealous for you with a godly jealousy, for I betrothed you to one husband, that to Christ I might present you as a pure virgin."
> 2 Corinthians 11:2

In case you missed it, Paul told these former perverts that, in the eyes of Christ, they are virgins! Unbelievable! Talk about having your body washed.

Only the blood of Christ can remove the stain of sin. If you're reading this and the enemy has been tormenting you about your past life, especially the sexual realm, then why not pray this simple prayer of faith right now?

Lord Jesus, you know all about my past life and the sexual experiences I have had. I'm truly sorry for defiling my body, and I ask you now to forgive me and wash my body from head to toe. Restore to me my virginity. I know you can and will.

Thank you, thank you, thank you. I receive your cleansing now.

Amen.

✝ SIX ✝

The High Cost of Forgiveness

We have looked at two amazing incidents of forgiveness. I trust you have found them encouraging. Forgiveness (cleansing) is God's gift to us through repentance and faith. As the old song declares:

Rock of Ages, cleft for me,
Let me hide myself in Thee;
Let the water and the blood,
From Thy riven side which flowed,
Be of sin the double cure,
Save me from its guilt and power.

Not the labor of my hands
Can fulfill Thy law's demands;
Could my zeal no respite know,

Could my tears forever flow,
All could never sin erase,
Thou must save, and save by grace.

Nothing in my hands I bring,
Simply to Thy cross I cling;
Naked, come to Thee for dress,
Helpless look to Thee for grace:
Foul, I to the fountain fly,
Wash me, Savior, or I die.

While I draw my fleeting breath,
When mine eyes shall close in death,
When I soar to worlds unknown,
See thee on Thy judgment throne,
Rock of Ages, cleft for me,
Let me hide myself in Thee.

While our forgiveness cannot be merited or earned, it does come at a price; a price so great that all the silver and gold in the world would not be sufficient to meet the cost.

PAYING THE PRICE

The first account of man's forgiveness takes place immediately after man's initial sin. Eve was deceived by the serpent into partaking of the fruit God had clearly forbidden them to eat. Adam, for whatever reason, went along with the whole chain of events and also partook from the tree.

Prior to this, it appears that Adam and Eve were clothed in *the glory of God*, somewhat akin to the way the disciples saw Jesus on the Mount of Transfiguration. But when our first parents sinned, they immediately became aware that they were naked — the glory had departed!

Filled with shame and guilt, they ran to hide and tried to cover themselves by their works. Ever since that time, man has sought to find ways to escape the feeling of being naked and ashamed of his guilt.

After being confronted by God, Adam and Eve were driven out of the garden but not before we read these words:

> "And the Lord made garments of skin for Adam and his wife and clothed them." Genesis 3:21

There's almost universal agreement among Bible scholars that for God to provide man a covering, there had to first be the *shedding of blood*. Tragically, that first sin resulted in a double death. The first being their own *spiritual death*, as promised by the Lord when he said, "From the tree of knowledge of good and evil you shall not eat, for in the day that you eat from it you shall surely die." The second death that day was that of the animal the Lord killed in order to provide Adam and Eve a covering.

Although we don't have all the details of this sacrifice, it's plausible that God allowed our first parents to see this innocent, spotless animal (possibly a lamb) being slaughtered and its blood poured out, all as a result of their own sin of disobedience. This would have had a profound impact on Adam and Eve as they saw this innocent lamb die in their place—knowing that the wages of sin meant death. It took the blood of the lamb to provide the atonement necessary for their sin.

Throughout the Old Testament the shedding of blood was the only acceptable sacrifice for sin. Only a spotless sacrifice was acceptable to God, as it was a foreshadowing of the ultimate sacrifice to come—the Lord Jesus Christ, the Lamb of God. For God to accept anything blemished, marred, or defiled would send the wrong message: that just anyone could die for your sin or mine.

Every sacrifice was a *type*, or *shadow*, the substance of which was Christ.

† SEVEN †

The Slain Lamb of God

*T*hank God that we no longer need to bring a spotless sacrifice to "church" in order to be cleansed or forgiven! While that's great news, it can also cause us to forget the high price that was paid for our sin.

Some time ago, while living in Florida, I listened to a young man expound on the way Jesus is revealed in Chapter One of the book of Revelation. Most of us are familiar with this amazing and glorious description. Jesus is portrayed as follows:

> . . . "one like a son of man, clothed in a robe reaching to the feet, and girded across His breast with a golden girdle. His head and His hair were white like white wool, like snow, and

His eyes were like a flame of fire . . . His voice was like the sound of many waters."
Revelation 1:13-15

This is by far one of the most detailed descriptions we have of our glorious, magnificent, Majesty—the King of kings and Lord of lords. What a day that will be when we stand in His holy presence and gaze upon Him, no longer through a glass darkly but face to face!

I believe that many Christians have this image in their minds eye when they envision that day, the day when time will be no more. What a day that will be! However, this wasn't the only vision John saw of our blessed Lord. Four chapters later, John described Jesus in a way that is often overlooked. Here is what he saw:

"I saw between the throne (with the four living creatures) and the elders a Lamb standing as if slain, having seven horns and seven eyes . . . And they sang a new song, saying, 'Worthy art Thou to take the book and break its seals; for Thou wast slain, and didst purchase for God with Thy blood men from every tribe and tongue and people and nation.'" Revelation 5:6,9 KJV

In this part of John's vision, he saw the Lord no longer in His blazing majesty, with eyes like fire and a voice like Niagara Falls, etc. Instead, John saw Him as "a Lamb standing as if slain." According to the Greek, the wording used here means to slaughter, butcher, or maim violently. One translation describes this as *a lamb with its throat cut.*

SLAIN FOR ME

In musing and meditating on this portrayal of Christ, as a lamb slaughtered violently, I couldn't help but think of the contrast between this record and the first. The first description is that of majesty, splendor, power, authority, etc. Here however, we see Christ as alive because he is said to be standing. This also implies He is now resurrected from the dead. Slain though, serves to remind us of the awful price He had to pay for your forgiveness and mine. In order to fully comprehend this graphic portrayal, we need to remember exactly what the Scriptures tell us about His suffering and death. We read in Isaiah 52:14:

> "But many were amazed when they saw him. His face was so disfigured he seemed hardly human, and from his appearance, one would scarcely know he was a man." NLT

Keep in mind He had already suffered greatly prior to His crucifixion. They had pulled out His beard, beat upon His head, lacerated His back by whipping, and finally nailed His hands and feet to the cross.

Little wonder Isaiah told us he was unrecognizable. John saw this awful picture of a lamb that looked like a *freshly butchered* lamb dripping in blood. Incidentally, the word *lamb* here is the Greek word which means a "little lamb" or "pet lamb."

Why do I draw your attention to this description of our Lord? Because I believe that throughout all eternity we will see both aspects of Jesus Christ. We will see Him as the great and mighty Lion of Judah, the King of kings and Lord of lords—now risen and reigning over all creation. And we will also see Him as the humble, suffering, servant—the Lamb who freely gave up His life in order to save us from our sin.

Without this constant reminder of His suffering, could it be that even in eternity we could lose sight of the incredible price that He paid in order to redeem us?

I'm reminded of the warning that God gave to His children before they entered into the Promised Land. Let me remind you what He told them:

> "Then it shall come about when the Lord your God brings you into the land that He swore to your fathers, to Abraham, Isaac, and Jacob, to give you, great and splendid cities which you did not build, and houses full of all good things

which you did not fill, and carved cisterns which you did not carve out, vineyards and olive trees which you did not plant, and you eat and are satisfied, be careful that you do not forget the Lord who brought you out of the land of Egypt, out of the house of slavery."
Deuteronomy 6:10-12

Even though it was God who provided His children with an abundance of blessings, including houses filled with good things, vineyards and olive groves, etc. God knew they could so easily forget the One who was the source of all their blessings. Was this the reason John was given this shocking image of Christ as a bloody Lamb, unrecognizable as a man? I believe we too will see Christ throughout all eternity as both the Lion and the Lamb.

As the hymn writer Jennie Evelyn Hussey wrote in her familiar hymn:

KING OF MY LIFE

King of my life, I crown Thee now,
Thine shall the glory be:
Lest I forget Thy thorn crowned brow,
Lead me to Calvary.

Chorus:
Lest I forget Gethsemane;
Lest I forget Thine agony;
Lest I forget Thy love for me,
Lead me to Calvary.

OVERCOMING the Enemy's Plans to Destroy Your Life

Show me the tomb where Thou wast laid,
Tenderly mourned and wept;
Angels in robes of light arrayed
Guarded Thee whilst Thou slept.

Chorus:
Lest I forget Gethsemane;
Lest I forget Thine agony;
Lest I forget Thy love for me,
Lead me to Calvary.

May I be willing, Lord, to bear
Daily my cross for Thee;
Even Thy cup of grief to share,
Thou hast borne all for me.

Chorus:
Lest I forget Gethsemane;
Lest I forget Thine agony;
Lest I forget Thy love for me,
Lead me to Calvary.

† EIGHT †
Amazing Grace

Now let's look into the doctrine of grace. We're all familiar with the word *grace*; the hymn "Amazing Grace" is said to be the most well known hymn in the entire world. It's been sung and played tens of thousands of times in both religious and secular settings; I've heard it at funerals, weddings, and a host of other events. But what do we really mean by the term *grace*?

As far back as the Apostle Paul's writings there were those who abused and used grace in a way God never intended. Grace can't be reduced down to one or two words. Its meaning is rich and vast. Here's how

Noah Webster sought to define it in his 1828 edition of his *American Dictionary of The English Language:*

GRACE
    1. Favor; Good will; kindness; disposition to oblige another.
    2. Appropriately, the free unmerited love and favor of God. The spring and source of all the benefits men receive from Him. *"And if by grace then it is no more of works." Rom 11*
    3. Favorable influence of God; divine influence or the influence of the spirit; in renewing the heart and restraining from sin. *"My grace is sufficient for thee." 2 Cor. 12:9*
    4. The application of Christ's righteousness to the sinner. *"Where sin abounded, grace did much more abound". Rom 5:20*
    5. Favor; mercy; pardon.
    6. Spiritual instruction, improvement and edification.

One thing stands out above all else regarding grace: it is entirely one sided. The *recipient* of grace contributes nothing whatsoever to it; grace is *bestowed*—it is not earned or merited.

RECIPIENTS OF GRACE

One of the most beautiful illustrations of this truth is found in God's requirement for building an altar. The altar was the place where man connected with

God. The altar was a place of reconciliation, forgiveness, worship, etc. According to "The Law of First Mention" we find God instructing His people that if they were going to build an altar, it could not be built with cut stones—only ordinary natural stones or even earthen clods. If man should attempt to place his handiwork on it by cutting or shaping the stones in some way, it would immediately profane the altar and render it useless. If or when someone built an altar to the Lord, he was instructed to build it of *earth* or *stone*, materials accessible anywhere. The lesson here, although much overlooked, is simply this: man cannot contribute anything to God's grace apart from the sacrifice itself.

How often we seek to contribute some of our own ability, talent, or merit, thereby priding ourselves in having earned or contributed in some way to our own forgiveness. But any attempt on our part to add to the altar immediately nullifies the grace of God. I want you to read it for yourself:

> "You shall make an altar of earth for Me, and you shall sacrifice on it your burnt offerings and your peace offerings, your sheep and your oxen; in every place where I cause My name to be remembered, I will come to you and bless you. And if you make an altar of stone for Me, you shall not build it of cut stones, for if you wield your tool on it, you will profane it." Exodus 20:24-25

When it comes to grace, there is nothing whatsoever that we can do to earn God's forgiveness. We receive forgiveness purely on the grounds of what Christ alone has done for us.

I'll never forget an incident some years ago when my wife and I were returning from a trip to visit our daughter, son-in-law, and four grandsons in New Zealand. At that time, I was travelling extensively while at the same time racking up the frequent flyer miles on American Airlines. One of the perks of being a frequent flyer was that on any outward-bound flight from the States I could use the American Airlines lounge free of charge. This meant that I could freely eat whatever was being offered, read a wide selection of magazines, watch television, and sit in a comfortable seat rather than being crammed into the seating at the departure gate.

Over the years I've often spent eight hours or more waiting for connecting flights, which is much easier with access to the airline lounge.

On this occasion my wife suggested we go to the American Airlines lounge; we had several hours to wait before our next connecting flight. I explained to my wife that I didn't qualify to use the lounge on inbound flights but only when leaving the States. You had to pay about $300.00 per year to qualify for inbound privilege; this allowed you to use any American Airlines lounge in the nation. Not believing me, my wife insisted that we try anyway.

I kept telling her they weren't going to let us in because once inside the lounge you are asked to show your ticket and airline card. Sure enough, the receptionist asked to see our tickets and then promptly informed us that we didn't have the right to use the lounge. I was just about to say, *I told you so*, when a voice behind me said, "I know these folks. Would it be okay for them to be my guests?" I turned to see an old friend standing directly behind us—John Paul Jackson, who we had not seen for several years. Paul showed the lady his ticket and his American Airlines card. The lady behind the desk immediately gave him her permission and welcomed us all to enter.

Many times since then I've thought about how that encounter exemplifies what Jesus Christ has done for us. We do not qualify to enter God's heavenly lounge—Jesus alone has paid the price. But He graciously bids us enter with Him.

PRECIOUS GRACE

One of the greatest mistakes we can make concerning grace is to treat it like water. Go into any building in America and you are sure to find an abundance of water. We have faucets everywhere, both inside as well as outside. We brush our teeth or wash our hands while the water runs freely down the drain.

Go to Africa, however, and visit some village where there is only one well, and notice how they value the water supply! Many villagers will walk miles to gain access to fresh water. Then they will walk miles home again with the precious water carried on their heads.

Sadly, the church in America has treated grace as though it were water, just another spiritual commodity we can use and even abuse if we like. Paul had to correct the church in Rome of this very thing. He wrote:

> "Shall we continue in sin that grace may abound?" Romans 6:1

They were treating grace as though God was happily dispensing it every time they chose to sin. They thought, *Why not sin? All I have to do is run to God's divine faucet and wash.*

This was never God's intention. Grace was God's gift for *if* we sin—not *when!* In fact, grace was God's gift *to empower us to not sin.*

In Paul's letter to Titus he wrote:

> "The grace of God has appeared, bringing salvation to all men, instructing us to deny ungodliness and worldly desires and to live sensibly, righteously, and godly" . . . Titus 2:11-12

POWERFUL GRACE

When we use grace as a means of continuing in sin, we are missing the point of grace. Not only that, we are grieving the Holy Spirit—or as He is referred to in the Book of Hebrews, the *Spirit of grace*.

Grace is a person—God Himself! He empowers us to resist and overcome sin, not to continue in it. When we realize that *grace* is a person, we begin to understand that it is possible for us to "insult the Spirit of grace." (Hebrews 10:29)

Our government provides millions of dollars every month in the form of food vouchers. These vouchers are freely given in the hope of helping needy families afford a healthier lifestyle. The program can improve people's lives, if used properly. But the sad fact is that many have abused this program and used the money for drugs, alcohol, cigarettes, or other harmful substances. Clearly this was not the government's intent when setting up the program.

Likewise, God never intended His grace to be abused and used for continuing in sin. In the Epistle of Jude, Jude reminds us to contend earnestly for the faith of our fathers. He then speaks about some who "turn the grace of God into licentiousness [unbridled lust] and deny our only Master and Lord Jesus Christ." (Jude 4) Here again we have a tragic example of the abuse of grace.

Let's not forget that forgiveness and grace are freely given to us by God. They came to us at the ultimate price of God sacrificing His only Son. Grace is not to be abused but to be *used!* His grace empowers us to resist and to overcome whatever difficulties we face—including sin and Satan.

GRACE TWISTED

In recent years, a distorted view of grace has crept into the Church; it opens the door for continual sin. The essence of the teaching is that all of our sins have already been forgiven—past, present, and future. In other words, your sins are forgiven before you even commit them. My answer to that is this: imagine a car dealership that provides every car buyer with a free car wash for as long as you own the car. You purchase a car and (along with the required paperwork) you are given a *free car wash* certificate. The dealer tells you that he has fully paid for all the car washes you will ever need, saying he believes that a clean car is the greatest way of advertising and promoting his dealership.

Several days later you innocently happen to drive down a muddy country road, full of potholes and ruts. Later, you notice your car is covered with mud, so you decide to avail yourself of your free lifetime car wash. But before you have time to drive through the car wash, your friends inform you that you no longer need to go to the car wash. They tell you that your first car washing was all that was necessary. When you tell them that you believe you *need* another wash, they say you're wrong. They say you've believed a lie.

You try to reason with your friends; you even show them your dirty car. They still refuse to acknowledge that the car needs washing. They inform you that what the dealer really meant was that once the dealership had purchased the car wash for you, it would keep the car clean forever. They also argue that to suggest it needs washing again is an insult to the dealer and the dealership. Your friends tell you, "When the dealer first paid for your car wash, that automatically washed the car for life; all past, present, and future dirt was washed away. Therefore, it never needs to be washed again!"

Such logic is usually considered ridiculous, ignorant, or crazy. Thinking back on your conversation with the dealer, you recall he said that *if* (not *when*) you happen to get your car dirty, the car wash would take care of it—and that he has a personal hatred for dirty cars; that's why he paid for a lifetime of free washes. He obviously never intended for you to drive around searching for dirty roads just so you could avail yourself of the car wash. That would be abusive to the car wash program and an insult to his dealership.

In a similar way, the atoning work of Christ paid in full for *all* of my sin. However, this doesn't exclude my need of repentance, nor does it give me license to sin. For my "friends" to tell me otherwise is totally false and misleading.

Sadly, this is the logic and essence behind the new *hyper-grace* message. This false teaching claims that all sins—past, present, and future—have already been atoned for; therefore there's no longer any need to repent. They say that would be tantamount to telling God you don't believe He's paid for all your sin.

This type of *fuzzy theology* falls apart for this reason: if repentance is acknowledging a sin that has already been forgiven, thereby making repentance unnecessary, then why do we tell people to repent the first time in order to be saved? If repentance is wrong *following salvation*, then (according to this "logic") repentance is also wrong *prior to salvation*. This erroneous type of teaching leads to even more false teaching, such as *ultimate reconciliation* or *universalism* (the false doctrine that says Jesus paid for all sin; therefore, all are saved).

The truth is that the *provision* for my cleansing was completed at the cross, but the *process* of cleansing is conditional upon my repentance, and not before.

✝ NiNe ✝
Examples of Forgiveness

*E*very parent feels joy when they see their children acting in a way they've been taught to. God is no exception. He expects His children to follow His leading and act *as He would* in each situation. This is especially true in the area of forgiveness.

Throughout His Word, we are instructed to *forgive*. God gave His people a number of illustrations of what forgiveness looks like. Here is what God said:

"If you see your enemy's ox or donkey wandering away, you shall surely return it to him."
Exodus 23:4

This might be easier to understand if you envision today's farmer who owns a tractor and truck. Both of these are invaluable to the farmer. Without the tractor he would be unable to plough, cultivate his fields, and then harvest them. Without his truck he would be devoid of transport, as well as not having the means to take his produce to market or take his family to church, etc.

Now keep in mind that, according to this scenario, you didn't do anything to instigate it; you're simply walking along the road when you notice your enemy's ox or donkey has broken loose and is heading in the wrong direction. Your initial reaction may be one of joy. After all, this is your enemy, the man who spread rumors about you, or who wronged you—perhaps he was responsible for hurting one of your children; or he refused to pay a debt he owed you, etc. Maybe you begin thinking this is God's way of repaying him for all he's done to you.

Being innocent of the whole situation, you might feel entirely justified in walking past the animal while thinking, *It serves him right!* Not only that, you might even envision him waking up the next morning and panicking at his loss; he would be utterly helpless without his two most important assets. However, God won't permit you to simply do nothing; God requires you to take both the ox or donkey and return them to your enemy.

A SPIRIT OF UNFORGIVENESS

The very next verse in this passage of Scripture paints another similar situation. We read:

> "If you see the donkey of the one who hates you lying helpless under its load, you shall refrain from leaving it to him, you shall surely release it with him."

Try to place yourself in this setting; you have just exited a farmer's market and you notice your enemy's donkey has collapsed under the weight of its load. The donkey is struggling to breathe, and you know that within a short time the donkey (if not released from its burden) will die. You, however, are not responsible for the donkey's plight. You did not overload the animal; you are simply a bystander.

You might initially feel sorry for this beast of burden, but the owner of the donkey just happens to be *your worst enemy*. This man has falsely accused you of all types of wrongdoing and destroyed your reputation around town. Could it be that God is getting even, on your behalf? If you're harboring a spirit of unforgiveness, the feeling of revenge settles upon you as you wait for your enemy to return for his donkey. If he doesn't hurry, his donkey will die! You hope he will be delayed . . .

Many people delight in witnessing their enemy's misfortune. However, God will not permit His people to harbor a spirit of unforgiveness! God instructs His people to immediately release the donkey from its load, thereby allowing the donkey to live and enabling their enemy to make a living.

One of the most misunderstood and misapplied scriptures regarding forgiveness is found in Proverbs 25:21-22 and in Romans 12:20. Here is how it reads:

> "But if your enemy is hungry, feed him, and if he is thirsty, give him a drink; for in so doing, you will heap, burning coals upon his head."

Many people interpret this as doing some act of kindness to your enemy so as to shame them, thereby making them feel bad (for whatever they've done to offend you). But is that consistent with how the Lord instructs us to act toward our enemies?

I think the best way to understand the meaning of the latter part of this verse is to imagine this is your only neighbor, who also happens to be your enemy. The weather suddenly begins to plummet to well below zero. Your enemy has run out of matches and is unable to light their furnace. Your enemy asks you for help. Here's your chance to get even and watch them suffer from the cold. Once again, you're not responsible for their lack of preparation; you feel justified in turning down their request. But God thinks differently. Your Lord tells you to provide the means whereby they can relight their furnace. This is the correct meaning; it is one of kindness and forgiveness rather than seeking revenge.

In Biblical times people would often carry things on their heads, as they still do in many cultures today. The burning coals would be equivalent to handing someone a box of matches. The live coals carried on the head in an earthenware pot would allow your enemy to rekindle his fire and thereby save his life. This would be especially true of herdsmen who would build fires to not only keep themselves warm at night but also offer protection from lions or other dangerous animals. Should their fire go out, they would make their way to the closest fire they could find hoping that individual would give them some of their coals to rekindle their fire. You get the idea!

Yes, our God is a forgiving God. While we were still His enemies, He sent His Son to die on our behalf, providing us with His undeserved love, grace, and mercy. Hallelujah, what a Savior!

† TEN †
Seventy Times Seven

As we've seen, the price for our forgiveness was not cheap. It cost Christ His life! He willingly bore the excruciating physical pain, as well as the utter humiliation of hanging naked on the cross in full view of His mother, disciples, and angry onlookers. Along with this (and mocking, blasphemous name calling, etc.) was added the *sin of the world*.

The writer of Hebrews refers to our salvation as "So great a salvation." This was only possible from *so great a Savior* and at *so great a price*. Let's never forget it. Paul writing to the Corinthians reminds them they were *bought with a price*.

In this chapter we will continue to look into the matter of forgiveness from a horizontal perspective. We've seen several accounts of forgiveness from the Old Testament, but now we will examine the words of Jesus to His disciple Peter regarding forgiveness.

We find the account in Matthew Chapter Eighteen. Peter came to Jesus with a question about forgiveness. We are told that *out of the abundance of the heart, the mouth speaks.* If this was the case, then Peter had been troubled about someone or something; he asked this question, "Lord how often shall my brother sin against me and I forgive him?" (verse 21) Peter then added, " Up to seven times?"

I'm convinced that Peter was looking for a slap on the back, or some other form of approval from the Lord for his repeated acts of forgiveness. But Jesus responded, "Not seven times but seventy times seven."

THE MERCIFUL

I can imagine the shocked expression on Peter's face. Jesus was not telling Peter that after forgiving four hundred and ninety times he could take revenge. Rather, Jesus was instructing Peter to develop a pattern, or attitude, of forgiveness. Once you repeat an action over and over again it becomes a habit, or at least it should. At this point, Jesus told Peter a story to illustrate how the kingdom of heaven operates.

Jesus told the story of a certain king who wished to settle the accounts of his slaves. One slave in particular had accrued a debt that is astronomical, some ten thousand talents. Since we are unfamiliar with *talents*, we tend to miss the enormity of the debt. This servant owed the equivalent of millions and millions of dollars!

The whole point of Jesus telling Peter this story was to show that there was no possible way he could repay his enormous debt. I can only imagine with a debt of this sum that sooner or later he knew his master would call him to account. With no means to pay, his master would be forced to take from him the most precious possession he had—his family.

Carrying this amount of debt, knowing that someday he would be called to account, the man must have been a nervous wreck. No doubt he spent his nights trying to imagine how he was going to handle the situation when the time came. His only solution was to plead for his master's mercy; without that, he was doomed.

When the time came, the slave did exactly that—he fell prostrate before his master, begging to be given more time. His prostration conveyed his need for mercy as well as his respect for his master's authority. Miraculously, his master was moved with compassion and released him totally from his debt.

He was, no doubt, stunned by what he heard. Perhaps he had thought, *If only my master will give me more time or reduce my debt by half.* But no, he was forgiven the entire amount!

Imagine how he must have felt at being released from so great a debt. I picture him arriving home that evening, taking his wife in his arms and swinging her around and around. Then he would sit his family down and explain what had happened. No longer did he have to worry about losing his children, his house, or his possessions; he would not be separated from his wife while serving prison time, etc.

The excitement must have been contagious as he informed his friends and neighbors that his debt had been forgiven.

THE UNMERCIFUL

Tragically, Jesus didn't end the story on such a high note. He explained that the following day this *now forgiven* man bumped into a man who owed him money. The debt was minuscule in comparison to what he had owed his master. Grabbing the man by the throat, the threatened to kill him unless he paid what he owed. The man fell down, pleading for mercy—but his cries were in vain. Rather than show mercy, the first man demanded to be paid back and had the other man thrown into prison.

By now the news had spread around the community of how the first man was shown mercy. Today it would make the headlines on the evening new and be the talk of the town. Unfortunately for him, his fellow slaves were watching. They ran and reported to their master how the man he had forgiven had treated his fellow slave. This time his master showed no compassion but outright anger instead. He rebuked the man for being so lacking in mercy toward his fellow slave.

Jesus then told Peter that his Lord handed him over to the torturers until all was repaid. If the story had ended there, we could assume that the real moral of the story was simply about forgiveness, and that rest of the story was just hyperbole. And in fact, many commentaries seem to gloss over the remaining verse. But we must consider and heed it:

> "So shall my heavenly Father do also to you, if each of you does not forgive his brother from your heart." Matthew 18:35

I can hear it now: *Are you suggesting that God can revoke our forgiveness?!?!*

Let me ask you a question: did the master, in the story that Jesus told, do that? Did he *revoke* his forgiveness? Yes, he did. And did Jesus say that His Father "would do the same"?

Yes, He did.

If this is true, we had better pay much more attention to our forgiveness of others.

† Eleven †
A Root of Bitterness

The story we looked at in the previous chapter was dramatic, to say the least. It was meant as a wake-up call, lest we trivialize the importance of our forgiveness of others.

One of my early mentors use to say, "We are all damaged goods." He meant that, over the course of our lives, we've known betrayal, abuse, disappointment, lies, back-stabbing, and a whole host of other things. We all have a story to tell, and yet seldom do we take the blame for any of it. This provides the perfect set-up for us to fight back, either verbally, physically, or perhaps internally and emotionally.

Since you're reading this book, I assume you're a believer and that you've experienced God's amazing grace in your life. Forgiveness, for the believer, is often taken for granted.

We can all look back in time to the place where we asked God to forgive us, the time that He became our Savior. We usually assume that our forgiveness is a "done deal" and cannot be revoked. If that was the case, then we could happily continue on with our Christian walk, without ever having to forgive others.

I must admit that would be extremely convenient. Then I could harbor all of the bitterness unforgiveness I desired. Jesus said it's easy to love those who love you, and that is the way the world operates. But then Jesus commanded us to love our enemies. This is only possible when the love of God is *shed abroad in our hearts* by the Holy Spirit.

TOXIC SOIL

After some 56 years of full-time ministry, I'm convinced that unforgiveness is the single greatest obstacle to personal revival, spiritual growth, and maturity. Unforgiveness ties the hands of God from working on our behalf. However, the moment we release another, we free God to work on our own behalf.

I vividly recall ministering at a large church in England some years ago. One morning I spoke on forgiveness. That evening one of the associate pastors introduced me to a lady who asked if she could thank me for my message. After she left, the associate pastor shared with me what she had told him.

This older lady had somehow slipped through their screening process and had been accepted as a student at the church's Bible school. There were a number of reasons she wouldn't have qualified, and she had some form of disability, including crippling arthritis. But following my message that morning, she had gone to this pastor and confessed that she had unforgiveness toward someone.

After she had confessed and they prayed together, she later returned to tell him that within a short time her arthritis had completely disappeared.

I believe that many sicknesses (though certainly not all) can be traced back to harboring unforgiveness. We are fearfully and wonderfully made, and what affects us spiritually or emotionally can also affect us physically.

I carry in my Bible a newspaper clipping dating back to 1999. The title of the article is "Dad: Revenge Led to Baby's Life, Death." It tells the story of a young couple who began dating and soon fell in love. Before becoming engaged, Amy (the young lady) decided to take a vacation trip.

While Amy was away on her trip, her boyfriend Ron lost his father. He contacted Amy, asking her to return and provide him comfort. Although Amy refused at the time, after her return they resumed their relationship.

The two were eventually married, and nine months later Amy gave birth to a son they named Tyler. Amy often worked late as a grocery cashier, and so Ron would get Tyler ready for bed at night. When Tyler was 7 months old (the night before Father's Day), Amy arrived home tired from work. Since the baby appeared to be asleep, she went to bed. The following morning, Amy found Tyler face down and dead in his crib.

The coroner ruled the death a case of SIDS or *sudden infant death syndrome.* However, two days after the funeral Ron told Amy that he had killed their son. According to his confession, he planned the crime even before they were married. He said it was revenge because of Amy's refusal to cut short her vacation when he needed her. According to the article (and I quote): "Shanabarger said he planned to make Amy feel the way he did when his father died. He married her, got her pregnant, allowed time for her to bond with the child, and then took his (boy's) life ... Shanabarger, 30, who begged officers to shoot him after he confessed Wednesday, was charged with murder ... Shanabarger said in his confession that on the evening of June 19, he wrapped plastic wrap around his son's head and face, then left the boy's nursery to get something to eat and brush his teeth. Twenty minutes later, he said, he returned, removed the plastic and placed Tyler face down in his crib before he went off to bed ... Shanabarger, who worked at a tire retreading center, told police he confessed because the image of his son's face, flat and purplish from rigor mortis, haunted him."

TOXIC HARVEST

Unforgiveness has an uncanny ability to morph into what you have just read. No one thinks they would ever stoop to this type of revenge, and yet it happens daily across our nation. Arguments quickly get out of hand, and rather than forgiving the person involved, they settle the score by gunshot.

We are reminded by the writer to the Hebrews not to allow a *root of bitterness* to spring up and cause trouble. Interestingly, in the very next verse he refers to Esau. You recall that Esau was the firstborn of Isaac, and the twin brother of Jacob. Esau not only sold his birthright for a bowl of chili but eventually lost his father's blessing, all due to his brother's cunning.

We're told that Esau shed many tears hoping for a way to recover his birthright. How often he must have sworn to get even with his brother; no doubt he would have killed him if it had not been for his mother Rebekah's wisdom in sending Jacob away to her bother Laban's house.

While we may not have lost a birthright, most of us can recall similar losses that we would give anything to regain. Think of how many young women lost their virginity due to a family member or neighborhood friend, or the number of young boys sodomized by a trusted friend or relative. The list of losses is endless, and so is the pain associated with each loss. If we don't find a way to heal these wounds, a deadly root begins to grow.

Some years ago, my wife and I returned to a home we had built in East Texas (thirty or more years earlier). At the time we built the house, I had planted some small pine trees; they were not more than a foot high. Some days later I decided to transplant one or two to another location. I simply pulled them up by the roots and transferred them to another area of the garden. Now, years later I was amazed at the size of the trees! They had grown some thirty or more feet high, with trunks 15-20 inches across. I remember looking at them and thinking I could never uproot those monsters, like I had thirty years ago. Likewise, unforgiveness can readily take root in our hearts and grow into a major stronghold.

But what do we really mean when we use the word forgiveness? In the following chapter we will explore this more in depth.

✝ TWELVE ✝
Letting Go

My wife and I spent five wonderful years in pastoral ministry in Gig Harbor, Washington; it holds a special place in our hearts. Not only is the city set in an idyllic setting, with its small fishing fleet and boats of every size and hew, but the flock we pastored was special in every way.

As the congregation grew, so also did the needs of the people. I discovered that several couples were receiving marriage counselling from a professional marriage counsellor. Word began to get back to me about how wonderful this man was, and how insightful and helpful he was to those seeking his advice. I began to probe a little and discovered that he was charging about a $100 per session. I knew this was way beyond what many in my congregation could afford, even though they also needed help.

So after hearing more good reports, I contacted this counsellor and asked him if he would be willing to come and hold a marriage seminar at our church. He explained that he was somewhat reluctant to speak to multiple couples at once, since each couple had their own unique difficulties. Not being willing to take no for an answer, I told him that there must be a number of issues that were common to all marriages. He agreed, and he said he would come, perhaps in part because I told him we would give him a generous offering.

When the day came, we had quite a number of couples show up anxious to hear for themselves what they had heard from others about this man. I too was curious to hear for myself what pearls of wisdom he might share that I could use to help others.

To my great surprise, he spent most of his time speaking about forgiveness. He stressed, over and over again, that we often tell our spouse, "I forgive you," when we really don't. Were just saying we've forgiven them to end the argument. He said we tend to file these grievances in our memories so we can use them again at some later date. What he said resonated with me as I had done exactly that.

He then shared a personal illustration: he told how he once had a particular model car that was increasingly hard to come by. You could tell by the way he referred to his car that it was much more than just a means of transport but rather a prized possession.

For some reason he had to sell the car, and afterward he regretted his decision. Some months later, he was parking his car and noticed to his surprise that parked not too far away was his "'old friend." He referred to his former car as being like an old coat that just felt comfortable to wear. Walking over to the car he said he was tempted to open the door and just sit in it one last time. He then made the statement that he had no right to do so because he had sold it. It was no longer his. "That's what true forgiveness is," he said. "It's letting go of your grievance, never to bring it up again."

We read in Luke 6:35-37:

> "But love your enemies, and do good, and lend, expecting nothing in return; and your reward will be great, and you will be sons of the Most High; for He Himself is kind to ungrateful and evil men. Be merciful, just as your Father is merciful. And do not judge and you will not be

judged; and do not condemn, and you will not be condemned; pardon and you will be pardoned."

The word *pardon* is used here is literally the word "to release." Forgiveness is *releasing someone* from whatever they have done to hurt or wound you.

Have you ever had one of those helium filled balloons that have a special message printed on them? You know that as long as you hold the balloon it remains under your control, but the moment you let go of the string, the balloon soars upward and cannot be retrieved again. This is what it means to release someone of an offense. Once you let go, you can never retrieve it or use it again against the person.

Going back to our marriage counselling seminar, the counsellor gave every one a blank piece of paper and told them to write on it the people who had offended them in some way. He then told them to bring their papers to the front and drop them in a garbage can. He likened their papers to the state vehicle registration paper of his old car, reminding them that once he had signed it over to the new owner, he had no right to it again.

His illustration remains with me to this day.

When we learn to release people, we too benefit by being released ourselves. Bitterness and resentment have a way of eating us alive or sucking the life out of us. Someone once said that *unforgiveness is like drinking a glass of poison in the hope that it will kill your enemy—only to find out that you are the one it kills.*

In the following chapter I want to share with you something I had never thought of before regarding forgiveness and the crucifixion of our Lord.

✝ THIRTEEN ✝
Father, Forgive Them

The writer of Hebrews refers to Jesus as "one who can be touched with the feelings of our infirmities." In other words, Jesus knew what it was to be rejected, wounded, hurt, betrayed, etc. He was fully man, as well as fully God. Therefore, He is our perfect High Priest.

When you study the life of Jesus from His earthly viewpoint, you soon realize that one of the greatest issues He had to deal with was His miraculous birth. While His virgin birth set Him apart from all others, it also presented Him with a major problem. To be born *out of wedlock* in those days was the ultimate stigma for someone to carry throughout their life.

You recall that the Pharisees said, "We were not born of fornication like you." Jesus was now some thirty years old and they were still calling Him a *bastard*. Talk about rejection.

Could He have faced this throughout His childhood and teen years? If so, then He had to continually forgive those who slandered and degraded Him publicly, as well as privately. I can imagine children in the neighborhood being warned by their parents not to play with Him as he was "born of fornication."

Immediately after He was anointed to minister, we are told He was led into the wilderness to be tempted by the devil. Following this season of temptation, we read that the devil left Him for a more opportune time. I'm convinced that throughout His adult life Jesus was under constant attack by the devil. We know that the Scribes and Pharisees were always looking for ways to embarrass Him or trip Him up on some point of Scripture. No doubt some of His most painful seasons were His betrayal by Judas, as well as Peter's denial of being one of His disciples. However, His greatest test was yet to come.

Before we look into that, let me take you back to what Jesus taught His disciples on the mountainside. Most biblical scholars refer to these teachings as "The Beatitudes" and consider them the most important of all teaching Jesus ever gave. In this series of teachings Jesus taught about prayer, and He gave us instruction on how to pray. This teaching, commonly referred to as "The Lord's Prayer," speaks about forgiving others.

I well remember Dr. David Du Plessis, also known as *Mister Pentecost,* teaching on this prayer; he made the point that it is one of the (if not *the)* most dangerous prayers you can pray. "Consider what you are praying," he said. "You are asking God to forgive you *according to* how you forgive others."

"And forgive us our debts, as we also have forgiven our debtors."

We all have a tendency to skip over certain truths because we've read or heard them mentioned so frequently; we fail to consider their importance. But Jesus underscored the matter of forgiveness again immediately following this prayer. He could have underscored other important points, like the Father's will or the kingdom, etc. Yet it was the matter of *forgiveness* that He focused on. Here's what He said:

"For if you forgive men for their transgressions, your heavenly Father will also forgive you. But if you do not forgive men, then your Father will not forgive your transgression."
Matthew 6:14-15

If we fail to obey this teaching, we do so to our own peril. This is so serious a matter that our eternal destiny depends on it! Which leads me now to another related teaching Jesus gave us in the previous chapter.

In this passage Jesus referred to an individual who had need of forgiveness from God and had secured for himself a lamb to present as a *sin offering*. (Keep in mind this instruction was given *prior to the cross*.) The sacrifice or offering had to be without blemish—spotless in every way. As he was waiting to come before the officiating priest to offer his sacrifice, he saw a brother who had something against him. In other words, their relationship was not as it should be, due to some problem, disagreement, or sin.

The man with the lamb wanted forgiveness from God for his sin, but now he was faced with this issue or sin that had come between him and his brother. Jesus did *not* say, "First get things right between yourself and God, and then when you have time, seek out and settle the problem you have with your brother." No! Jesus said:

> "Leave your offering there before the altar, and go your way; first be reconciled to your brother, and then come and present your offering."
> Matthew 5:23-24

Once again we see how Jesus placed the forgiveness of others as a top priority and as a requirement for our own forgiveness.

With that thought in mind, let's fast forward to Jesus and the time of His crucifixion. Jesus had just been betrayed by one of His own (Judas), and Peter had denied Him. Pilate examined Jesus and found Him innocent of the charges laid against Him, but he reluctantly handed Him over to the demands of the Jews.

Prior to this, Jesus was severely beaten; His back was lacerated like a ploughed field; His beard had been pulled out by the roots and His head beaten—while he wore a crown of thorns. By this time His face was unrecognizable and the pain indescribable. Stripped naked, Jesus was nailed to the cross, while the crowd cried, "Away with Him!" and "Crucify Him!"

Imagine the pain and humiliation He suffered. Then imagine the weight of the world's sin being laid upon Him. Remember, Jesus was not immune to physical and emotional pain. He was *the man* Christ Jesus. In His darkest hour, when the whole world turned against Him, He cried out, "Father, forgive them for they know not what they do!" I believe in the Greek it implies that He *kept crying out*, "Forgive them!"

Why do I bring this to your attention? Most, if not all, who are reading this are familiar with this incident. After all ,it's the *grand finale* in the life of Jesus; the completion of His earthly mission. He told us that He was *born to die.* Theologians refer to this as "The Atonement," the very climax of our Lord's mission — not to mention the very core or crux of our Christian faith: *the cross.*

But wait a minute! Have you ever considered what would have happened if Jesus had never uttered the words, "Father, forgive them?"

Remember what Jesus taught about the man bringing his offering to the Father, and the Father telling him to first be reconciled to his brother? Well, here we have the same exact scenario. Jesus isn't bringing a spotless lamb as a sin offering; He is the spotless Lamb. He's offering Himself for the sins of the world. But in order for His offering to be accepted, He has to be first be reconciled to the very ones who rejected Him and were responsible for His intense agony and suffering. In other words, if Jesus had died with unforgiveness toward His brothers, and had never uttered the words "Forgive them," His Father would have had to reject the sacrifice of His own Son, and the whole atoning work of the cross would have been in vain. We would still be in sin and without hope in this world. Take a moment and consider that.

I personally believe this was the devil's final attempt to thwart God's plan of redemption. Jesus was fully man and could have easily allowed resentment and bitterness to creep into His heart for what they were doing to Him. But He chose forgiveness so that you and I could not only experience God's forgiveness but also extend that forgiveness to others.

As I bring this study to a close, would you take a minute to examine your own heart and see if you are holding onto any resentment or bitterness toward someone? But first, allow me to interject here several quotes by three prominent authors and teachers. I believe their words will have far greater weight than mine due to their spiritual stature. The first is from Oswald Chambers, author of *My Utmost For His Highest*. This devotional classic has impacted the lives of countless believers for generations:

> "The Forgiveness of a child of God is not based on the ground of the atonement of our Lord, but on the ground that the child of God shows the same forgiveness to his fellows that God his Father has shown him."

The second quote is from Dr. Martyn Loyd-Jones:

> "I say to any man who is imagining fondly that his sins are to be forgiven by Christ, though he does not forgive anyone else. Beware, my friend, lest you wake up in eternity and find Him

saying to you—depart from Me; I never knew you."

My third quote is from R.C. Ryle, taken from his book *The True Christian:*

> "The gates of heaven are broad enough to receive the worst of sinners but too narrow to admit the smallest grain of unforsaken sin."

As you can see, these great men of God understood the importance of forgiving others if we ourselves are to be forgiven. With this in mind I encourage you to pray:

Dear Lord Jesus,

Please give me the grace to forgive _____. I release him/her for what they have done to me. I ask you to bless them and reveal yourself to them. With your help I will endeavor to speak of them with grace and mercy from this day onward.

Now, Lord, I'm asking for your forgiveness for my sin of bitterness, resentment, and unforgiveness toward him/her. Please forgive me, and replace my bitterness with your love and grace for him/her.

In Jesus name I ask.

Amen

www.ingramcontent.com/pod-product-compliance
Lightning Source LLC
Chambersburg PA
CBHW010854090426
42736CB00019B/3450